LONELY AMERICANS

Photograph from Dry-point in Freer Gallery
JAMES MCNEILL WHISTLER

LONELY AMERICANS

by
ROLLO WALTER BROWN

*"It isolates one anywhere to think
beyond a certain point."*

Essay Index Reprint Series

BOOKS FOR LIBRARIES PRESS
FREEPORT, NEW YORK

First Published 1929
Reprinted 1970

STANDARD BOOK NUMBER:
8369-1699-9

LIBRARY OF CONGRESS CATALOG CARD NUMBER:
74-121452

PRINTED IN THE UNITED STATES OF AMERICA

Preface

I have written about these individualists because I liked them.

R.W.B.

Contents

CHAPTER		PAGE
I.	An Olympian	15
II.	Whistler and America	51
III.	A Listener to the Winds	89
IV.	An Adventurer Out of the West	127
V.	A Self-Indulgent Apostle	165
VI.	Cosmic Prospector	199
VII.	A Sublimated Puritan	235
VIII.	Lincoln the Radical	261

Illustrations

James McNeill Whistler	*frontispiece*
	PAGE
Charles William Eliot	22
Edward MacDowell	94
George Bellows	134
Charles Eliot Norton	174
Raphael Pumpelly	206
Emily Dickinson	238
Abraham Lincoln	262

Acknowledgments

IN writing these sketches, I have used, in addition to first-hand knowledge of my own, two distinct kinds of information. The first is the printed material—letters, reminiscences, memoirs—that is taken for granted as a source for the writer of biography. It would seem but pedantry to set down in bibliographical lists all the material of this kind that I have looked through for significant facts; but I wish to express my gratitude to many painstaking editors who have helped make material of this kind a matter of library record.

The other kind of information—and I have drawn upon it heavily—is the unpublished material that men and women who chanced to have an interest in the subject-matter of this volume have generously contributed. Since this material by its nature cannot anywhere be a matter of printed record, I wish to make specific acknowledgment to all those who were good enough to offer it for use:

ACKNOWLEDGMENTS

To Mrs. John W. Alexander and Mrs. F. Van Vorst Sleeth for much that pertained to Whistler; to Mrs. Edward MacDowell for the unrestricted use of the private papers of Edward MacDowell, and Dr. Charles H. Cutler for a record of MacDowell's long last illness; to Professor Joseph R. Taylor for George Bellows's record at Ohio State University, Mr. Robert Henri for material of great variety on Bellows in New York, and Mrs. George Bellows for a body of intimate letters and jottings of her husband; to Dr. W. F. Melton, Mr. Leonard L. Mackall, Mr. George H. Browne, Professor George Herbert Palmer, Dean L. B. R. Briggs, Mr. David T. Pottinger, and Professor Paul J. Sachs for letters or for other personal material relating to Charles Eliot Norton; to Mrs. Elise Pumpelly Cabot, Mrs. Margarita Pumpelly Smyth, Professor Henry Lloyd Smyth, Professor Ephraim Emerton, and Mr. David McCord, for similar material relating to Raphael Pumpelly; and to the late Mrs. Henry S. Lane for a body of information concerning Henry S. Lane and Abraham Lincoln, Miss Helen Elston Smith for letters from

ACKNOWLEDGMENTS

the correspondence of Henry S. Lane, and Professor S. E. Thomas and the late Judge John Maxwell Cowan for accounts of Lincoln-Douglas debates.

I wish also to thank Mr. William C. Lane, Librarian of the Widener Library, and Mr. Walter B. Briggs, Assistant Librarian, for the use of the Henry Villard collection of letters, the Charles Eliot Norton treasure collection, and for unexampled thoughtfulness about many matters; the Art Association of Concord, Massachusetts, for the use of a letter that Whistler addressed to his mother; the Freer Gallery for the use of the Freer collection of clippings on Whistler, and for transcripts of certain material.

R.W.B.

I

An Olympian

AN OLYMPIAN

I

It is difficult to think of Charles William Eliot as a human being. He was some sort of remote superman, was he not, who lived and acted quite beyond the scale of ordinary mortals? His years stretched well through three-quarters of the nineteenth century and quite through the first quarter of the twentieth. Only six of the twenty-nine Presidents of the United States had completed their terms of office before his birth; he had lived three years before Victoria became Queen of England; and he was almost ready to enter college when gold was discovered in California.

He lived when there were no railroads to speak of, no telegraph, no practical use for electricity, no scientific laboratories in the colleges, no surgery worthy the great name; and when a confessed belief in man's ultimate ability to talk over a wire or to fly in the air was often enough sneered at as proof of insanity. But he lived also when aircraft were circling the North Pole; when men were talking not merely over a wire but through the ether; when surgeons were performing the most delicate operations on limbs and brain; and when scientists were looking through solid substances with a new light in a way that in his early life would have been regarded as a defiance of the Creator. To the young who look upon the Victorian Era as just within the horizon of history, and who cannot remember the sky when there were no airplanes in it, the mere span of his life seems little short of eternity.

In like manner there is a seeming limitlessness to what he accomplished. He helped to develop the entire current system of elementary and higher education in America; he was prominent in establishing the beginnings of what to-day is regarded as modern medicine and modern science; he was the chief instrument in changing his own institution from a provincial college to one of the important universities of the world; he participated in every struggle in behalf of greater respect for human beings from the days of negro slavery to the fight for a World Court in 1925. Between eighty and ninety, when most men are in their graves and forgotten, he was in the thick of the struggle for all sorts of great causes in American life. In that last decade alone he published one hundred and ninety-two articles on important questions—and writing for the press was only one of his many means of making himself felt!

Little wonder that this record should amaze his contemporaries and disciples! But is there not something interesting in the human being from whom so much has emanated? Just what manner of man was it who experienced so much and contributed so much? If the record itself is astounding, might there not be something deserving of brief consideration in the personal method and the personal life of the man by whom the record was made?

2

It is not possible to approach an understanding of President Eliot without bearing in mind that, despite his persistent activity, he was much alone among men. It is true that his loneliness changed in quality as he passed through the succeeding phases of his life; but he never escaped it. Despite his intimate and loyal friendships, he somehow was a man apart.

In his earlier years—in truth, until he was well past what many men regard as middle life—his loneliness was that of a fighter who has the odds against him. In his later life, when the long stretch of years had healed the wounds of battle, he often spoke with mock-seriousness about those combative days: "No, I was never lonely; I always had a fight on my hands!" But when he was serious, his reference to them was different. "Can you fight?" he asked a young professor who had gone to him with a disconcerting problem.

"Why, yes," the man replied; "that is, I think I can."

"Can you fight when you are in the minority?"

"I have done so occasionally."

"Can you fight when everybody is against you—when not one man is ready to lend you support?"

"I am ready to try it if necessary."

"Then you need have no fear. But if you have convictions, it will sometimes be necessary to do no less."

His willingness, even readiness, to engage in combat was stimulated by at least two sets of circumstances. In the first place, there was something in his appearance in youth and middle life—and to a lesser degree in old age—that induced antagonism in certain people. He was near-sighted—"no oculist has ever been able to procure for me full vision"—and moved about with head aloft in seeming disregard of other people; and the prominent birthmark on the right side of his face distorted his upper lip into a suggestion of superciliousness. For some reason, boys on the Boston Common enjoyed "belting" this aristocratic, arrogant-looking contemporary, and—perhaps for the same reason—he enjoyed giving them in return everything the occasion required. In college he was known for his persistence and his toughness of fiber. As a young tutor at Harvard he was known for the same qualities. One year, among the undergraduates there were not enough oarsmen to make up a crew for the City of Boston Regatta on the Charles. So they called upon Eliot—there seems to have been no occasion up to that time to invent eligibility rules—and he responded. He was tall and slender then—according to the records of the regatta he "weighed in" at one hundred and thirty-eight pounds—but he did his full share in winning the six-mile race—"six miles with three turns"!

Concerning his power as a teacher there were different opinions. But by the time he was thirty-five—he was then professor of chemistry at the Massachusetts Institute of Technology—it was proposed to make him president of Harvard. Much opposition developed. Some of his opponents said that if he were made president they would henceforth have nothing to do with the institution. He would wreck it with his over-aggressive, cold-blooded methods! There was doubt as to whether his nomination would ever be confirmed. At the very same time his wife lay dying. Heartbroken and alone he walked the streets, caring little whether he was made president or not. But his appointment was confirmed.

When he assumed the presidency he seems to have made every effort to reveal the catholicity of his views. His inaugural address—October, 1869—would still constitute an excellent school for college administrators. But the situation which confronted him in his new office called for heroic treatment, and he was not the one who would hesitate to administer it. So with a reputation already established for enjoying a fight, and with a situation at Harvard that required many changes if the institution were to command the respect of the world of scholars, he very soon had a worse reputation for pugnacity than he had before he took up his duties. Many, to be sure, found assurance in his clear-sighted activity; but when the professor in the Medical School asked him why so many changes had to be made, and he replied, "There is a new president," many others were only convinced anew of the high-handed methods the new president meant to employ.

So he moved about in a world that was chiefly hostile. "In all the early part of my career as a teacher and an educational administrator," he said in an address before the Massachusetts Historical Society a few months before his ninetieth birthday, "I was much engaged in controversy, not to say combat, and that at home as well as outside of Harvard. In all my public appearances during those years, I had a vivid sense that I was addressing an adverse audience." At home many of the members of his own faculty derided him and his educational schemes; students—some of whom later were made members of the faculty and became his staunch supporters—enjoyed poking at him the kind of fun that carried a sting; and in the outside world pretty nearly everybody welcomed an opportunity to make him a target. "One of the painful recollections of my life," one of his lifelong friends once said, "was to see men lying in wait for him and assailing him whenever he appeared in an educational meeting." To all the

Photograph by Notman

CHARLES WILLIAM ELIOT

other reasons for denouncing him, the friends of Yale added yet one more by showing how Yale had not—at that time—adopted Eliot's pernicious system of letting college students choose their own course of study. Wherever he went he was grimly serene in the consciousness that most of the people around him were at heart his opponents.

That he was able to survive this stormy period—which reached into the last decade of the nineteenth century—may be attributed to two or three qualities of his character. He was tenacious. In his later years he confided to younger men that he believed much of his success in combat resulted from his ability to turn aside at once when he was utterly blocked, and take up for the moment some simpler struggle where the promise of victory was greater; then, when he had learned more strategy and had regained confidence in himself, to return to the major struggle, often enough greatly to the surprise and consternation of his adversaries. When he was once convinced that the idea for which he struggled was an essential one he did not often accept defeat.

Another quality which enabled him to survive was his loftiness. He did not become embroiled in little affairs. He insisted that every struggle in which he participated should be conducted on a high level. There was nothing insinuating in his method; he was not afraid to carry a position by frontal assault. He abhorred cunning, and he did not need it; for he was strong. Once after a lively session of the Harvard Board of Overseers, he good-naturedly reminded one of his friends on the board, "Why did you not come to my support when you saw so many against me?" The friend replied, "It was such good fun to see you flatten them out one by one, yourself."

In such struggles he was generous in hearing opposition and was ready to be convinced by it. But whether or not he was convinced, he gave his opponents a full hearing. When he advocated that college students under certain circumstances should be allowed to graduate in three years, he met strong opposition in the faculty. Whether he was moved wholly by a generous fairness, or partly by a boyish readiness to give every advantage and prove that he could still win, he gave the opposing members the use of the university printing press in order that they might have every facility for combating his cherished scheme. . . . It must have been only his high sense of fairness; for at the end of the year, with these men's destinies in his hands, he promoted some of them to full professorships.

When men came close to him, moreover, whether as opponents or as allies, they found in him another quality which added to his ability to survive. He was, despite the casual observation that he was a hard and cold New Englander, a man of profound emotional experience. He suffered deeply when he suffered, and he enjoyed deeply when he enjoyed; and he had the great range of sympathy which goes with depth of feeling.

Early he was left with a family of children by the death of the first Mrs. Eliot, and for some years—some of the stormiest of his public career— he had to be not only president of Harvard, but father and mother in his own household. Then he met the spirited and beautiful Miss Hopkinson who was to become the second Mrs. Eliot—and he proved to be just as aggressive a suitor as he was a college president. How could it matter what the watchful ladies of Cambridge thought? He marched erect and in full view along Garden Street carrying a bouquet of flowers to the fascinating young creature!

She was beloved by her friends as a singer of unusual charm and as an irresistible mimic. When she became the second Mrs. Eliot she had her part in developing qualities in her husband that the less discerning had failed to detect in him at all. They began the day by singing: by singing hymns; by singing—according to veracious guests—the most orthodox hymns! They rode bicycles together—until President Eliot was well past seventy. They entertained their old and young friends in great simplicity and in great good humor. On Christmas Eve they welcomed the Harvard students who were so far away from home that they had to remain in Cambridge over the holiday season. No one who was a guest at one of those evenings can forget the group that gathered round the fireplace, with President Eliot warming his hands in rapt silence, Mrs. Eliot beaming with sly good humor, and Charles Eliot Norton, stooped with age into a great curve, reading with restraint and beauty the Gospel story of the birth of Jesus.

Mrs. Eliot put him through the paces of a happy, objective, and not too serious life. To the end of her radiant days she whimsically corrected him when he did not see according to her standards of humor. After the international celebration of his ninetieth birthday he was recounting with delight all that had taken place at the meeting. "But do you know, I couldn't hear a word of Peabody's prayer." With sunshiny humor Mrs. Eliot observed, "He wasn't speaking to you, dear!"

Beneath the austerity which his years of combat accentuated, she knew him to be full of the great tenderness once so generally ascribed to women. When stern college discipline was required he could enforce it; but he often did so with tears in his eyes. On one occasion when his conscience told him that he must support one of his deans who had dismissed from college the son of a widow who appeared at the president's house in her son's behalf, he finally withdrew from the conference. Later Mrs. Eliot came to explain that he was so moved he feared he could not talk. He was a sound sleeper; he boasted in his old age that he could go from the stormiest debate late at night and be lost in sleep in a few minutes. Yet occasionally when he arrived at University Hall in the morning he admitted that he had been unable to sleep for thinking about the tragic misfortune of young So-and-so.

That he was able to survive his long period of combat is not, then, mysterious. Most men are chicken-hearted; a tenacious man overawes them. Most men who undertake a struggle lose themselves in bickerings and in hot debates over nonessentials; a man who keeps his head high and refuses to turn aside to enjoy the transient satisfaction of putting his adversaries in the hole, very soon finds that his fellows are looking to him for guidance. Most men expect an adversary to be without sympathetic understanding; a man full of tenderness for fellow-mortals—unregenerate though many of them be—takes away their cherished basis on which to oppose him. Sometimes it becomes an honor to know such a man, even if the acquaintance has come through opposing him.

3

"Do you suppose anybody ever called him Charley?" one man asked another as they talked about his serene loftiness at seventy. Perhaps, they thought, the second Mrs. Eliot may have done so, since she was always taking liberties with him. Still, as they turned the question over, even that seemed improbable. He was too much of a lawgiver to be thought of trivially. These two men had the greatest affection for him—one of them, greater affection than for any other man he had ever known—and they turned to him for counsel on every sort of problem. Yet they found it difficult to think of him as anybody's intimate.

Their feeling revealed the position occupied by President Eliot in his late middle life and earlier old age. His full height, his magnificent gray head, his deep, sensitively modulated voice, his firm but easy bearing, commanded profound respect. He had fought through many stormy years, and had developed a circumspect manner of looking at things. He had come to possess a rare capacity for disengaging not merely the essential things, but the things that give life its color, its bloom. So, despite all else that he did in this period, he came to be looked upon as a very august man who stood in a high place and dispensed wisdom on many matters. Not that he refrained from entering energetically into the affairs of the hour! But it was not in his character to participate in anything as a mere equal. He participated as a benevolent St. Bernard would enter into the play of puppies. Wherever he chanced to be, he towered above his associates.

Many people said he uttered commonplaces as though they were oracular. His adversaries—and he still had plenty of them—protested that he thought himself infallible. They invented such pleasant instances as "President Eliot says, 'I think it shall rain this afternoon.'" They asked if there might not be found somewhere one tiny instance of his being very, very slightly in error. Nevertheless, it is doubtful whether any man continued to be consulted on so many diverse matters. The education of little children; the best places to invest small sums of money; the merit of this or that long manuscript—on chemistry, philosophy, education, poetry; the thing to do when the son of a millionaire marries the daughter of a boarding-house keeper in Cambridge; the internal affairs of China; the training of ministers of the gospel; freedom of speech; the education of the Negro; landscape architecture; the study of music and art in colleges for young women—with countless matters of such variety his days and much of his nights were taken up.

When he dealt with such matters there was in him a trace of the impetuous warrior, but of the warrior who has fought his way to a point of vantage. He stood in good-humored composure before a hostile audience of laborers in Faneuil Hall —the chairman promised punishment for any delegates who indulged in catcalls while President Eliot spoke!—and explained just why he was opposed to picketing. He dealt with the picturesque, electric Theodore Roosevelt, President of the United States, precisely as a vigorous grandfather would spank an obstreperous ten-year-old boy. He stood before theologians and told them of the religion of the future and why it would "make Christ's revelation seem more wonderful than ever to us." He prepared—with aid—a five-foot shelf of books which he said would provide a liberal education for the men and women who mastered them. When architects and building committees could find no suitable inscriptions for public buildings and other monuments, he provided something lofty and enduring.

In truth, the great dignity and gravity with which he said everything led many to believe he had no sense of humor. He had. Often he revealed the subtlest humor. But, as some one once observed, his humor was "unreliable." He was not pliant in the hands of a given occasion. There was sometimes a chasm between what the occasion would seem to call for and what President Eliot actually uttered. When a brilliant young scholar, about to be added to the teaching force at Harvard, was led to him for presentation and was fearful that his scholarship might not bear the unwonted strain, President Eliot bowed, and with grave serenity said, "I am very happy to meet you. But you are not large."

"No," the young teacher admitted, "I am not very large."

"Are you vigorous?"

"Why, yes; I believe I am stronger than my size indicates."

"Do you take exercise in the open air?"

"Yes, I walk several miles every day."

"It is a very excellent thing for a young man to do. Good-morning!"

But with all his top-heavy seriousness, men came to recognize in him the elements of greatness. He had rounded into that period of active life when a man's contributions are beginning to stand revealed—if they are probably ever to do so. Men began to sum him up, to speak about what they had seen him do. They had seen him change the Harvard Medical School from a careless institution where students attended instruction only four months in the year and were obliged to pass in only five chief departments out of nine—with deadly results for patients—into one of the important schools of the world.* They had seen

* *President Eliot's own version of an incident in the reform of the Medical School (Harvard Memories, pp. 31-33):*

"The hour of taking the final vote on the acceptance of this plan by the Board of Overseers approached, when suddenly Mr. Charles Francis Adams, who had recently returned from rendering a very great service as Minister to England from the United States during the Civil War, said to me, 'Whom shall I put into the Chair?'—he was President of the Board of Overseers—'I wish to speak.' I had not the faintest idea on which side of the hot debate Mr. Adams was going to speak. He had uttered no word during the three meetings which had already been devoted to it. But he soon stepped out on the floor, and as he began to speak, it was evident that he was much stirred. There was a fierce glare in his eyes, and his face grew red as he told this story:

"'I think it is high time that the Harvard Medical School should be fundamentally changed. A young graduate of the Harvard Medical School established himself in my town of Quincy a year or two ago, and was getting along quite well in practice. But one day it was observed that an Irish laborer, to whom he had been called, died suddenly, and unexpectedly to his family. Nothing was done about it, for the family did not pursue the subject. Then another laborer, a granite-cutter in Quincy, suddenly died under this young man's care; but again him convert the Harvard Law School into an institution of which an eminent foreign jurist said, "It is without equal in any land." They had seen him, an amazing judge of men and a person unmindful of petty enmities and prejudices, surround himself on all sides with scholars of distinguished ability and great personal power. They had seen him become a strong ally in the development of a more adequate education for women. And atop all, they had seen his despised elective system—despite all the abuses to which it is open—go to

nothing came of it. One day the wife of an American mechanic saw her husband, who had not appeared to her to be very sick, suddenly become comatose; and in great alarm she told the young doctor that she wanted an older physician. The oldest physician in Quincy was called in; and when he looked at the patient he said to the young physician, "What have you done for him?" To which the young physican replied frankly, "I have given him so much sulphate of morphia." "Well, doctor," the older man replied, "you have killed him" —which turned out to be the case.'

"Mr. Adams told this story and added, 'Now, I suppose this young doctor was one of those graduates of the Harvard Medical School who were required to pass only five examinations out of nine to obtain the degree. I am in favor of the proposition which has come to us from the Corporation.' The vote was taken almost immediately, and there was a strong majority in favor of reform in the School. Till that moment I had not felt sure that there would be any majority for it."

every part of the country and become a means of liberalizing men's thinking.

There were, moreover, less official achievements. He had enforced upon the world a theory about the sacredness of every man's work; a ditch-digger might become a "minister" if only he put enough character into his digging. He had been the chief American figure in making parents and teachers and school committees see that a boy experiences vastly more of the educative process when he works at a subject in which he delights. He had given to religion a new vigor through abundant fresh air, and to science a touch of the sacredness of religion. He had been largely instrumental in winning the fight for greater social health throughout the country. He had become the accredited daily illustration of the effect of a serene spirit on physical health. And he had with great labor established in men's minds one thought which all the intolerance of a post-war period cannot wholly dislodge; namely, that professors in universities must have the right not merely to think but to express their thoughts; that the way to develop a great university is not to badger men into playing safe, but to place faith in their loyalty to the high pursuit of truth.

Could anyone except a great man make all these contributions—and many more? Those who once ridiculed him and his ideas did not now protest when he was referred to as "the first citizen of the state," and later "of the nation." Why should not men turn to him for counsel? Merely a glimpse of him as he walked erect and at peace with his own spirit was enough to reveal an extraordinary man. A student who had gone to Cambridge from an obscure village in a remote part of the country said, a dozen years after, that it was worth all the money he ever spent in Cambridge just to see President Eliot come from the little red-brick house on Quincy Street, glance about in the morning sunshine with the admiring reverence of a child, walk to University Hall, respond with amused but benevolent dignity to the salutation of the negro boy who gathered cigarette stubs, and then, very erect, mount the steps and disappear in the building.

There was another informal proof of his accepted greatness: men were beginning to use him as a justification for reasonable conduct in daily affairs! "I was a sophomore," a man said twenty years after college, "and I had a sophomore's notions of what constituted fitness. I would not have been seen crossing Harvard Square with a package of groceries in my arm for any sum of money. In the course of the long vacation I chanced to be in Cambridge. The day was sweltering. Just before lunch time I passed the large grocery store formerly in the Square. I heard a familiar voice and looked up. President Eliot was coming from the door with an enormous watermelon under his arm. He moved off in the direction of Quincy Street. At a distance, I followed. Halfway home he put the melon down against the roots of an elm, took out his handkerchief, and mopped his brow and cheeks. But he did not rest long. Evidently somebody wanted that particular melon for lunch. So he lifted it to his arms again and moved on toward the house.

"Nothing that Harvard College ever did for me

was worth half so much as that five minutes of President Eliot's life. For he knocked out of me all the nonsense there was in me—and there was a great deal!"

Yes, there had been changes since the days when every audience he addressed was an "adverse audience." If by chance he paid the street-car fare of some Italian woman who had lost her nickel—as any man might be expected to do—the incident was good for several inches of space in the newspapers. People liked to say that a Symphony could not begin without him. And to have him present at a wedding was scarcely less an honor than being married in the presence of the Pope!

Yet there remained in him a lofty inscrutability that discouraged intimate approach. The multitude did not try to hobnob with him. They wanted to see him, but they were content to peer at him through the wrought-iron fence of the College Yard. Even among the graduates of his own university, among men who now respected him, admired him, and sometimes loved him, there was an inclination always to appoint a committee, or name a delegate, to bear their greetings to him. He was a very wise, very good man, they felt, and he could offer the most acceptable counsel to be found anywhere. But it was not easy to feel that he entered instinctively into the everyday tribulations of his less sternly self-disciplined fellows.

4

As he traveled majestically into his latter eighties, the loneliness he experienced was of a new kind. The "adverse audience" of his youth had given way to an eager audience; the restraint of a public that admired his wisdom but never sought to become intimate with him gave way to warmth and an affectionate pride. Yet he was lonely.

He was still a fighter; he still gave out oracular wisdom; but he was a mellow old man who no longer aroused antagonism or induced restraint. A few people, it is true, maintained an attitude of bitterness toward him, and still contended that he was the greatest single disintegrating force in

American higher education. But the overwhelming majority looked upon him as a prophet; or if not a prophet, at least one of truth's very high priests. Men delighted in his benevolent attitude toward everyone and—some of them—were ashamed to think that they had not discovered it before. They pointed to him as the great example of a man who could change his mind with scrupulous honesty if he thought the evidence warranted it. He stood before an audience in the First Parish Church of Cambridge—when he was eighty-nine—and stated that all through his forty years as president of Harvard, and for many years thereafter, he had believed that a layman should not represent the church publicly. But in view of the present needs of the church, he had become convinced that he had been wrong, and he wished to make a declaration of his change of belief. He decided that, despite all the good fellowship and poetry surrounding the use of wine—he had as president always served ice cream and sherry at the traditional meetings of the Divinity School faculty—it were better as a social-health measure to have national prohibition; and he was heard without being called either a Puritan or a fanatic. All else was lost in admiration for a man who could change his mind when he was nearer ninety than eighty.

In this period he ceased to give all of his thought to the future, and became pleasantly reminiscent. More than that, he confessed one day to his oldest associate in the Harvard community that he enjoyed the experience. He welcomed undergraduates to his house and told them about the early days. Occasionally he accepted invitations to sit with them in their own informal meetings, and delighted them by the hour.

As he turned more and more to his past, he found that other men were doing so—affectionately. One day a visiting lecturer at the university passed Memorial Hall on his way to lunch, and noticed many automobiles parked on every side. He slipped into the theater and found President Eliot—then nearly ninety—standing before a large audience, his head aloft, his hands clasped, and his thumbs moving steadily, while he discussed a problem in education. The visiting lecturer had not talked with him for a half-dozen years. So at the close of the meeting, while President Eliot waited twenty minutes for an automobile that was to carry him to a luncheon, the two sat alone on the stage in the high-vaulted, quiet theater and reviewed many matters. When they were ready to go, President Eliot said, "My age has affected my knees just the least bit; so if you don't mind, I believe I'll take your arm while we go down the steps."

They marched down the steps together and toward the exit, the visitor proud to have the magnificent nonagenarian firmly grasping his arm. As they stepped out into the sunshine, the visitor said to him, "When I was a student I used to enjoy seeing you on your way to work in the early morning, and I often thought I should like to tell you. Of course, I never did; but I want to tell you now."

President Eliot smiled, bright-eyed with a pleasure the visitor had never seen expressed in his face before. "Do you know," he said, for a moment half lost in sublime retrospection, *"that* is the great joy of living to be an old man. Not a few Harvard men have said much the same thing to me within the past few years. If I had died at seventy or eighty, I should have missed all that."

These expressions of a more intimate affection on the part of younger men became more numerous until they culminated in the national—even international—celebration of his ninetieth birthday. It is doubtful whether a private citizen had ever before been honored with a meeting of such official brilliance and spontaneous good will. It is doubtful whether any man in any station ever received such an outpouring of expressions of high regard. He was delighted that there was nothing "mortuary" about it all, and entered upon his part with the enthusiasm of youth. He not only spoke at some length to all the assembled friends and dignitaries, but went a little later in the afternoon to the College Yard and there addressed the thousands of students assembled to do him honor. To the students he spoke with a vigor and cordiality scarcely surpassed in his most resolute years—he advised them not to wait too long to marry! Then he went to his own house and engaged in a less inclusive celebration there.

He had come into his own, had he not? On every hand he was told of the fruits of his long labors. Every public appearance was an ovation. Graduates referred to him affectionately as "a great old boy." People stopped and watched in wonder and admiration when he stepped cautiously but with a trace of the old vigor from his automobile and entered the First Parish Church.

But his contemporaries had gone. The gracious, beautiful Mrs. Eliot slipped quietly away into the shadows. With a few—very few—exceptions, all the people around him were younger—much younger—than he was. He sat in the long study upstairs and conferred with men about chemistry and the scientific mind; about the rehabilitation of agriculture in Bulgaria; about international good will; and, with great concern and enthusiasm, about the religious life of college students. But he could not move abroad so readily as he once could. And most of the men who came to see him knew little of the times he knew best and loved most.

In a new way, then, he was a man apart. People talked about him as if he were a very great, very benign curiosity; how old he was when their grandfathers were born; how long he had taught mathematics and chemistry before Darwin started all this discussion of evolution; and why he never went as ambassador to the Court of St. James. Good Cambridge ladies said, "It would be nice if he could die now before he becomes too feeble. It must be dreadful just to sit and wait!"

But he had been alone before, and he could wait. When men came in from their rushing, excited world to offer their respect, he was full of questions, stories, arguments. Was a man to give up his radiance of youth simply because he chanced to be a little past ninety? Just to know that there were still so many young fighters in the world was beautiful, very beautiful. When his eyes had become dim and his hand too palsied to hold a pen, a friend sent him a volume—just off the press—in which he had quoted from Whittier's lines to Oliver Wendell Holmes. President Eliot asked his secretary to send his thanks. "Tell him," he said:

" *'Yet on our autumn boughs, unflown with spring,*
  The evening thrushes sing.' "

So he sat and waited. Occasionally there were flashes of the old will, the old impetuosity; there were so many things that ought to be done; but there was not strength. Then the serenity came again. It was something, was it not, to have fought so valiantly and, all in all, so successfully? It was something, was it not, to have contributed of one's best judgment so generously? It was something, was it not, to have men everywhere speak of one with grateful affection? Could one hope for more of what he himself had modestly called "the fortunate circumstances of life"?

So, much alone, he waited.

II

Whistler and America

WHISTLER AND AMERICA

I

It was a strange chapter: the most brilliant American genius of his day living year after year in London, always with one eye on his own country, yet always unwilling to return. The record of his fellow expatriate, Henry James, is more readily comprehensible. Henry James was peering about with æsthetic caution for traces of civilization—searching for some safe retreat for his precious spirit. These traces might, perchance, be found in Europe rather than America, since Europeans had longer been engaged at doing their best—and worst. He looked vainly in England after he had looked vainly in France. Disillusioned, he began to wonder if, after all, they might not be found with least searching in America. Before he settled down in England as a British subject, he came back to make the final inventory. But James McNeill

Whistler, whose concern in the world was to get a significant view of anything that possessed interesting vitality—why did he remain a citizen of the United States, yet never come back for so much as a casual hour?

It was not because he loved England. To him England meant Ruskin—the Ruskin who insulted him by writing about his "Nocturne in Black and Gold": "I have seen, and heard, much of cockney impudence before now; but never expected to hear a coxcomb ask two hundred guineas for flinging a pot of paint in the public's face." England meant the exasperating details of the suit which Whistler brought for damages; it meant his discovery that more people were with Ruskin, in both opinion and sympathy, than he had suspected; it meant that he, a dapper little person from somewhere west of the Atlantic Ocean, had to sit in a courtroom filled with mirth at his expense and hear Baron Huddleston ask concerning his "Battersea Bridge," "Which part of the picture is the bridge?"—and the stinging laughter that followed; it meant hearing Burne-Jones testify, "A picture ought not to fall short of what has been for ages considered complete finish," and, when asked if this picture revealed the finish of a complete work of art, "Not in any sense whatever"; it meant hearing Tom Taylor, the art critic, testify that Whistler's pictures were only "one step nearer pictures than a delicately tinted wall-paper"; it meant enduring the titter that went over England when, after the testimony was all in, Whistler received a verdict for damages to the amount of one farthing.

England meant, too, the prolonged battle with the Royal Society of British Artists; it meant the eventual estrangement with Leyland because Whistler's conception of the Peacock Room constantly enlarged as he worked, and Leyland refused to enlarge the price as much as Whistler demanded; it meant—though the trial was in France—the enervating days of the suit that Sir William Eden brought to recover either Lady Eden's portrait that Whistler had painted or the money that he had paid to Whistler "as a valentine," and Whistler's unsuccessful effort to broadcast his somewhat favorable verdict by publishing *The Baronet and the Butterfly;* it meant the gilded jibes of Oscar Wilde, who became so sharp in his spite that Whistler declared Oscar was at last becoming original; it meant, from the time his "White Girl" was rejected for the exhibition of 1862, a more or less constant flood of nasty criticism, such as —"the periodical inflictions [a Whistler exhibition] with which this gentleman tries the patience of a long-suffering public!" Who could say that he kept away from America because he loved the British? England was the native land of "the enemy." His affection for the country was summed up when he hoped that not one of his paintings would ever hang in a British national gallery.

Nor did he hate America. True, he did make sarcastic remarks about Lowell, Massachusetts, the city of his birth (1834). True, also, he was dismissed from West Point—because, he never hesitated to explain, he had declared silicon to be a gas, and the professor, in his advantageous position, had thought otherwise. "If silicon had been a gas, I would have been a major general!" Yet he never ceased to look upon West Point as one of the chief places of the earth. While he was there he made sketches that the Military Academy was glad enough to exhibit to the public after he had become a figure in the world. He designed the cover for the "Song of the Graduates," 1852. He sent a copy of "Whistler vs. Ruskin" to the West Point library. He rejoiced to the end of his days in the West Point spirit. When he was wrecking London dinner parties by calling upon heaven to give the Boers an eternal victory over England, he was sure they could have it if only they had a few West Point men to help direct their patriotic armies.

He was proud, too, of American products. When certain Americans, noisily abroad, rushed up to him and spoke of a common nationality, he could be ashamed, wrathful, or contemptuous. But he was proud of a good American. And he was even boastful about his fellow countrymen's ingenuity. "Just see this! Just see this!" he exclaimed to Mr. and Mrs. John W. Alexander one day. Then he stood for ten minutes on the stairway and exhibited the intricacies of a cane umbrella—the first one he had ever seen. "Look at that; and that; and that! It is perfection, what! Made in New York—New York! That's the way they do things over there."

Nor was he himself un-American in temperament. On the other side of the Atlantic they found in him all the chief American qualities—especially the disagreeable ones. "The enemy" in England were pleased to refer to his "transatlantic impudence"; in his readiness to use his fists they could find nothing European. In France—where criticism is nothing if not logical—he was a typical American. Jean Tharaud once set forth some of the details. Whistler conformed to the American type because (1) he was bored with the resources of American life; (2) he possessed the American's refined feeling for advertising, and understood "how to organize his reputation"; (3) he had an American's practical instinct for recognizing the limits of his genius—he saw clairvoyantly that he possessed "more grace and taste than invention, more subtlety than strength, more reflection than spontaneity"; and (4) he loved human activity rather than the quiet of nature—he painted not the drowsy landscape, but the faded faces of Venetian houses bearing the wrinkles of long life, the busy Thames, the dockyards of Liverpool, the Luxembourg Garden, and especially the human face that "bears the stigma of a living passion or the regret of one now past."

Whether or not this list of "American" qualities is comprehensive, it would be difficult to make Whistler temperamentally more at home among Englishmen than among Americans. Yet in 1886 he had this experience: His friends had urged him to send to America an exhibition of his work. Major Pond, manager for many celebrities on the American platform, wanted him to come over and lecture. In London the year before, he had startled his friends as well as "the enemy" when he delivered his "Ten O'Clock." Such a man, Major Pond thought, might catch the fancy of the American public. Whistler was favorably inclined. He directed John W. Alexander to select the pictures that were to be included in the exhibit. But before the plan could be carried into execution, he began to waver, became fearful, and finally refused to proceed. He had tried to visualize the reception that he and his pictures would have in New York; he had tried to anticipate the response that his "Ten O'Clock" would elicit from an American audience. That he might have less success in New York than he had had in London seemed possible. The risk of such a calamity as falling short in the land of his birth threw him into a mild panic from which he demanded the one sure escape—remaining where he was.

2

In this he acted with the shrewd vision which startled the casual-minded throughout his life. He wished to be accepted in America as a distinguished son. But certain American attitudes of mind precluded any such happy acceptance. For one thing, he was a dandy; and the American people have never been willing to take a dandy seriously. They will tolerate, even worship, a man who sedulously cultivates carelessness of manner, but they will waste no time on a man who is over-zealous in appearing well groomed. The pseudo-Lincolns will always get more votes than the pseudo-Washingtons, no matter what the question at issue. The clamor is for "two-fisted" persons and "he-men," even if the two-fisted persons are bullies and the he-men are cowards. If put to the test, Whistler might have engaged in combat with a two-fisted person and sent him to the mat early in the first round. But such a possibility would have made no difference. He was a slender, dapper window-model of a man, with a tall, stafflike cane, low-crowned, broad-brimmed hat, overnice curls, and actor-like movements that attracted children and adults when he passed through the streets. How much of a chance would he have had in Pittsburgh, Indianapolis, Buffalo, or Chicago?

Likewise he knew that America had not yet learned that the artist may be a person of intellect. Talk for five minutes in any miscellaneous assemblage and you may discover that the artist is still thought of as outside the pale of important-minded persons. An artist may be skillful, he may be a master of some technique, he may know how to drape models or hang pictures; but have the people ever thought of elevating artists to responsible positions? John La Farge might well have been in the United States Senate; a hundred years from now he might stand as one of the reassuring glories of nineteenth-century political life. To-day it would be refreshing to see Mr. Cyrus Dallin, Mr. Charles W. Hawthorne, Mr. Charles H. Woodbury, Mr. Robert Henri, or a dozen others, made members of the Upper House—not merely because they might save the city of Washington from being overrun by equestrian statues, but because they could bring to national affairs an intellectually honest approach, a habit of considering the entire scene, and a willingness to experiment disinterestedly that would expedite the nation's business—and save taxes! But does anybody propose to put them there? An artist in Congress? An artist anywhere where brains are required—or at least desired? Entrust our destinies to a group of smart prestidigitators? Whistler knew that he had not the slenderest chance of being accepted in the United States as intellectually competent.

Just as certainly there was another guarantee of misunderstanding. He believed in the aristocracy of perfected ability; his fellow countrymen professed faith in God-given common sense. Now on some matters there is no reason why one intelligent man who lives among men may not be as competent as another. An Iowa farmer may have as trustworthy an understanding of human motives as a man of the same intellectual grasp who lives anywhere else. But there is an elementary distinction between good judgment in affairs of human conduct—in which all men by necessity have some practice— and the expertness required in carrying out a program of scientific education, in planning a city, in maintaining an art center, or in conceiving and painting a picture. This elementary distinction Americans are still hesitant to accept. In some parts of the country, commissioners of education and city engineers are elected by popular vote; in some cities, pictures for art galleries are chosen in the same manner. It was in such a competition that George Bellows once declined to participate by writing: "Does the public also vote on disease in Montclair?"

Now Whistler not only set artists above the untutored; he set them above art critics! Toward all those who did not know art from the inside, he had been baited by the England of John Ruskin into assuming an exaggerated attitude. "The scene," wrote Oscar Wilde when Whistler delivered his "Ten O'Clock," in London, "was in every way delightful; he stood there like a miniature Mephistopheles mocking the majority! He was like a brilliant surgeon lecturing to a class composed of subjects destined ultimately for dissection, and solemnly assuring them how valuable to science their maladies were and how absolutely uninteresting the slightest symptom of health on their part would be." Still, in Ruskin's England there was need of a picturesque presentation of Whistler's theory. The artist is superior. He sees elements for use that the dull of eye pass unnoticed. He lives, therefore, in a world apart. He is a spiritual aristocrat—in degree according to the singularity of his genius. But could Whistler hope to have his theory of the essential aristocracy of artists received with fervor in America?

3

All his doubts were corroborated. With a few stalwart exceptions, Americans did not think of him as a person of sublime intent. Did not his *Gentle Art of Making Enemies* appear in 1890 and prove in his own words that he was a cad and a bag of light fustian? What other kind of man would air his petty quarrels—with full annotations—on the open pages of a printed book? What other kind of man would dedicate a book "To the rare few who, early in life, have rid themselves of the friendship of the many"? And did not the newspapers give report of his preoccupation with trivialities—at best, trivialities—in London and Paris?

Occasionally some American defended him. At one stroke such a champion could reveal his own solitariness and the content of mind of Whistler's detractors. In 1892, after the French Government had purchased Whistler's "Mother," one such indignant champion wrote to the New York *Tribune*—from London: "He is our countryman, and though art may not have a country, artists have. Mr. Whistler, I am certain, would claim no favor because he is an American. But are we Americans to be silent when a great distinction is bestowed upon an American artist? Are we to cavil at it? Are we to malign him because Mr. Ruskin did? Are we to prefer the caprice of an English critic to the considered testimony of the representatives of a great nation, infinitely superior in knowledge of art to the nation whom Mr. Ruskin has been lecturing for two generations on its blindness and ignorance? Are we to say that the Luxembourg is not much of a show because it finds room for an American? Have we so many great American artists that it is worth while to discredit the one who is most esteemed abroad?"

But Whistler the etcher, or Whistler the painter of "Mother," "Carlyle," "Battersea Bridge," "La Princesse du Pays de la Porcelaine," "Lillie in Our Alley," "The White Girl," "The Blacksmith of

Lyme Regis," "La Mère Gérard," "The Yellow Buskin," "The Little Blue Bonnet," "Portrait of F. R. Leyland," "Portrait of M. Théodore Duret," and the like, was not in the minds of most Americans. Here is the Whistler—the newspaper Whistler—they liked to amuse themselves with:

"Mr. Whistler sat in his palatial studio trimming his cuffs. His historic white forelock was neatly done up in a brown curl paper, signifying that he had as yet received no visitors. On his easel was a stretch of virgin canvas which Mr. Whistler looked at now and then, frowning. All at once he sat up in his chair and hurled his scissors through an open window. From the street there presently came a howl of rage, at which Mr. Whistler smiled with evident satisfaction.

" 'Ha,' said he, 'not yet nine o'clock and another enemy made. Not bad.'

"Then he began slowly to take down his curl paper. 'Still,' he remarked, kicking off his slippers and moodily regarding the holes in his socks, 'still—I can think of nothing to paint.'

"As if in answer to his complaint, there came

a knock on the door, and a servant stuck his head in, dodged a small jardinière, and stuck his head in again.

" 'Mr. Tinlot, of the United States,' said he."

And then a column or two of what took place between Whistler and the "Hon. Dicky Peachblow Tinlot" of "Pinochle Palace, New York."

Nor were the newspapers alone in caricaturing him. One of the "smartest" articles about him appeared in *McClure's Magazine*, entitled "Whistler the Painter and Comedian." A footnote gave an account of his work as a painter, and the text of the article considered the comedian. At times the writer—who withheld his name—became insolent. He said that Whistler's Sunday afternoons brought together "the sort of menagerie that could but rarely congregate at the same time anywhere else." The article revived the story of how Whistler and his model had once decided to commit suicide by jumping into one of the canals of Venice, but how after they were on their way to the canal they chanced to meet some acquaintance and forgot to complete their journey. It told how he dyed his hair black except for the famous white lock which "on grand occasions is tied up with a small ribbon" —this despite the fact that the lock was white prematurely, and left the rest of his hair black; a singular white lock that other members of the Whistler family have had. It unearthed the lines written by the wag when Whistler had been overtaken by financial misfortune:

"Of various 'arrangements' we've had an array—
Black and white, gold and silver, tawny and gray;
But of all the arrangements there yet remains one,
And that's to arrange with the troublesome dun."

Everything had to be interpreted for the worst. His sharpness of wit—and Whistler stories, most of them good ones, had to be syndicated so that everybody might have a little of his sharpness—was not wit; it was egotism. When, according to report, an admirer gushingly assured him that there were only two great painters, "you and Velasquez," and Whistler replied, "But why drag in Velasquez?" or when another assured him that she had just been down along the Thames and that it was almost like a series of his brilliant etchings, and he responded, "Yes, nature is creeping up!"—was he not merely employing an acrid coating of whimsical color to disguise his own exalted opinion of himself? In a land where men openly profess expertness in questions of the humorous, everyone wanted to make him serious when he was not!

Even when somebody essayed to consider his intellectual pretensions, there was abundant likelihood that he would not receive the benefit of the doubt. The New York *Sun,* as late as the time of his death, referred to him as having been a conspicuous figure in the intellectual depravity of England that ended in Oscar Wilde—a movement characterized as "unbridled egoism" and "intellectual dishonesty." "Nothing that he ever wrote will bear the test of a sane or wholesome analysis." And as for his work as an artist, the *Sun* recognized the merit of his etchings and a certain "very few" of his paintings, and then concluded: "Of all the rest, with Whistler dead and no one to explain them and continue the cult, the less said the better."

It was so easy to keep on thinking of Whistler the freak, the madcap; so easy to think of him as a flaneur who flitted lightly, who created occasions for advantageous combats, who drank unceasingly of the coarsest dregs of a decadent world. When Du Maurier began publishing *Trilby* as a serial in *Harper's Magazine* with Joe Sibley as such an evident caricature of Whistler that Whistler demanded the suppression of the issue then current, and the publishers thought the American edition of the magazine quite beyond control, nobody in America seems to have regretted that Du Maurier's "unwhiteness" was to have a lease on life until the story should appear in book form with a colorless substitute for Joe Sibley. Had not Du Maurier hit off the real Whistler? Was not Whistler getting what was coming to him? In order to keep on talking about this Whistler, the facts of his life were unnecessary. A Chicago newspaper interviewer quoted the vice-president of a powerful bank as having said: "One of the brightest things he ever did, it seems to me, is a sketch, in writing, called 'Ten O'Clock.' It consists entirely of quotations from Philip Hamerton."

No one should take away the Whistler they cherished—not even death. "One of the fine things," said a St. Paul newspaper, "that have transpired about Mr. Whistler since his death—we hope the leakage does not disturb his repose—is that at one time he aspired to save his country! Phenomenon, but we have to believe it.—Think of it. Whistler, the eccentric, living according to rule. Whistler, the æsthetic, molded into garments like those of a regiment of other men." Hard enough to believe! Hard enough to believe that Whistler ever aspired profoundly to anything! And it required no effort at all to keep on speaking casually about "Spitfire Jimmy," "studied insolence," "unscrupulousness of the egomaniac," and "decadent artificiality."

4

Now this playboy was not the essential Whistler; it was only the Whistler he had learned to use advantageously in a world filled with "the enemy." He must tell nothing, lest he unwittingly let "the enemy" close to his thoughts. Walter Crane, for instance, admired Whistler's work genuinely. He had gone to one of his private views, and he hoped to develop an acquaintance that had there a frail beginning. But he was known to associate with men included among "the enemy." So when he later came face to face with Whistler at a masked ball and greeted him expectantly with "I believe we have met before," Whistler replied with dry finality, "Very likely!" Or if he did not remain silent he must put them on a false scent. If they wished to see Whistler the eccentric—and they evidently did—very well, just let them look. In the course of an evolution from a bright schoolboy to a dapper gentleman of sixty, he mastered the makeup of the external Whistler with a perfection unrivaled. But never did he laugh with such a devastating crash as when somebody suggested that he was an unfathomable genius chiefly interested in social give-and-take and the glare of the footlights, but casually interested from time to time in turning aside and striking off a masterpiece or two.

When the sociological conditions were right, the essential Whistler could be expected to appear. Not often, certainly. He lived in a world presided over by such an arch-enemy as Ruskin. But there were people to whom he could speak without bravado. "My own dearest Mother: I have not written to you for years, it seems to me, and at last I have fallen into an utter silence; but yet I think of you continually, and wish always to go down to you and tell you how I love you and am always your fond son." Jimmy filled with remorse? But to those who would persist in thinking of him as only a model bad boy, his reason for not going was more astonishing still: "I waited, though, and have waited all along, that I may get the better of my work and be able to come to you and say that I am at length free and happy in the result of my labor." She shall have an opportunity to rejoice with him, as she sees him "produce lovely works one after the other without any more of the old agony of doubt and uncertainty."

Whistler a worker! Whistler so intent upon painting that he neglected everything else! Was he not merely living up to his reputation by pulling the wool over his mother's eyes? Whistler in the agony of doubt or uncertainty—about anything! Was he not just covering up his irresponsible genius?

Yet here is the essential Whistler. Here is the man he hoped the cultivated minority would detect. Being an artist was the one serious concern of his life. That half-pleasant, agonizing experience brought everything else to the level of nothing at all. He drove sitters frantic with his exactitude. He worked until he became limp. He worked again as soon as he could recover the feeling that genius would help him. Members of his own family marveled at his capacity to get work done at all sorts of mysterious times. What he struggled toward was seeing—seeing clearly, honestly. Always he hoped to see with the directness of an unclouded approach; always he was about to rid himself of the confusion that results when memories and preconceptions enter too largely into seeing. He hoped in a lifetime to see Venice and the Thames. So valiantly did he endeavor that he almost led the people of England to see! It is not an easy matter. Earlier in the century John Ericsson had invited the British Admiralty down to the Thames to see a new iron boat propelled by a kind of windwheel submerged at the stern. The representatives of the British navy looked, but could not see. Whistler, despite the heavy opposition of Ruskin, was more successful. The British public laughed at what he said he had seen, and then looked again in order that they might laugh some more, until in the process some of them actually began to "see Whistlers" through the twilight over the river.

Just as industriously he struggled through a long self-discipline to his final originality of expression. Was there not something to learn from the Japanese? He would find out. Was there not everything to learn from Velasquez? He would learn as much from the divine master—until then too much neglected—as reverence and devotion would make possible. Were not the stories or "sentiments" that nineteenth-century British art revealed cheap and absurd? He would break up the old conventions by painting "arrangements" that would tell all—or at least tell enough—without any sentimental tags. It was an exacting business. One must be master of one's spirit, one's world, and one's medium.

Late in life he believed that at times he had achieved this mastery. The clear, reflective intelligence of his father and the austerity of his mother sometimes showed through all the whimsicality of his work. "Whistler the rare, the weird and extravagant magician, the isolated and bewildering genius," wrote Camille Mauclair, making notes at the Whistler exhibition in Paris in 1905, "has vanished. We simply behold a great painter, as we have beheld so many others. Our vision is perfectly clear: we see what he has imitated, whence he has borrowed, his hesitations, repetitions, the slow evolution of his originality. We see how much he worked, doubted, labored: very human it is, very beautiful. We are astonished, but we love him all the better. We feared lest adoring one subtle thing two hundred subtle things might prove monotonous or mutually detracting. On the contrary they help strengthen one another. The mind is enthralled by the energy of his style; and what an atmosphere of earnestness and purity there is! The logic, the health, the discipline of this artist-mind are self-evident to all of good faith. . . . In the formidable and supreme trial he holds his own."

His young disciples, too, in the intimacy of the studio, felt in him the vitality of the artist. "I was well into my work," wrote a young woman fresh from the United States to become a pupil in the Académie Carmen, where Whistler had consented to act as critic, "when the clatter of Carmen's wooden shoes began downstairs, and up came Whistler's dear old model—always little Carmen to him. Her stage whispers electrified us. 'The Master! He is coming! He is here!' Down again Carmen ran for her husband, Tordo, whom she ordered to 'go at once' and stand at the street door, while she came up again, dragging her great breadth and thickness, breathless with excitement —the while, smoothing her apron and arranging the ribbon in her hair. 'He is here! The Master is here!'—at the same time holding back the curtain and curtesying.

"Those of us who had been sitting arose and stood as immovable as wooden soldiers. No entrance could have been more dramatic. I shall never forget it.

"There stood the small, spare figure, looking seven feet tall, all in black, holding with a gloved hand his straight-brimmed very high silk hat against his chest, a monocle resting uneasily under a heavy brow. His thick hair was gray and even in color, having absorbed in the process of time the white lock that was made much of in his younger days and in the caricature of him in the original version of *Trilby*. His mustache and imperial were worn after the manner of the French painters of the day, but not to the point of eccentricity. His cheeks sagged with sorrow or weariness, but his eyes expressed neither—they were keen, critical, giving out a challenge. 'What for? We shall see!' He had a metier to foster; an Art that had become his belief, his religion."

Not that he was pedagogic. He could display as hot a whimsicality in offering criticism as he ever displayed at the dinner table. "With whom have you studied?" he asked a pupil whose palette Whistler suspected of showing the influence of William M. Chase, whom he hated—in his later life. "Why," she replied, "with Emil Carlsen and Amédée Joullin."

"And with Chase, perhaps?"

"Yes, for one month, en route to Paris."

Whistler turned on his heel. "I don't know him!"

He could play the actor, too. One day when his monocle slipped from his eye while he lectured informally, and rolled across the floor, a dozen ardent disciples rushed to rescue it from the dust and bread crumbs. He deigned not to touch it, but with an easy flourish drew a fresh one from his waistcoat pocket and adjusted it in his eye as he proceeded with the lecture.

But the artist was dominant. His criticism came from a knowledge of art that was from the inside out. There was the "sanity of genius" in what he said. There was something of the same sympathetic sanity in his manner of speech. Before an easel where a frightened pupil had done poorly, he was silent for a moment—dapper, yet not wholly unsympathetic—and then observed in friendly fashion: "It's a long road!" He wrote out for his pupils propositions which have the restraint of permanent documents. He deplored the tendency to heighten every effect until "scarcely a feature stays in its place, so fierce is its intention of firmly coming forth; and in the midst of the unseemly struggle for prominence, the gentle truth has but a sorry chance. . . . The Master from Madrid himself, beside this monster excuse of mediocrity, would be looked upon as mild. 'Beau, bien sur, mais vieux jeu!'" If only people would see! But they "never look at Nature with any sense of its pictorial appearance—for which reason, by the way, they also never look at a picture with any sense of Nature, but, unconsciously, from habit, with reference to what they have seen in other pictures. . . . Could the people be induced to turn their eyes but for a moment, with the fresh power of comparison, upon their fellow creatures, as they pass in the gallery, they might be made dimly to perceive—though I doubt it, so blind is their belief in the bad—how little they resemble the impudent images on the walls! How 'quiet in color' they are! How 'grey'! How *'low in tone'*! And then it might be explained, to their riveted intelligence, how they had mistaken meretriciousness for mastery, and by what mean methods the imposture had been practiced upon them."

The artist seeking the gentle truth.

5

Now it was the difference between the attitude of Britons and the attitude of Americans toward this essential Whistler—Whistler the artist—that made him content to remain away from his own country. Britons might not like him, they might not fancy his paintings or etchings, they might call him a most unperfected artist; but they did, even in their spitefulness, think of him as an artist of some kind. They derided him. They kept honors from him that were his due. They fought him with a narrowness of spirit that will always be a discredit to British fairness. But, wrong as they were, they did fight him on the basis of art. There was a certain intelligence in their wrong estimate. Not only that. They eventually began to admit his importance—so openly at times that he himself declared the atmosphere was a little less glacial. There was nothing sudden, therefore, in the warmth of recognition expressed in England at the time of his death—and every provincial daily newspaper as well as the metropolitan publications had something to say. There was much evidence of respect; there was often enthusiasm; and occasionally there was righteous indignation. The *Academy* declared that "no man of our time was so incontestably the artist." The *Morning Advertiser* asked: "Why, if Whistler was the greatest painter of our day, did he win no official recognition?" Then at considerable length it demands an explanation of Whistler's dying plain Esq., instead of R.A., or A.R.A., or Lord Whistler like Lord Leighton. Eventually—though late—England as well as France had come to think of Whistler not only as an artist, but as a great artist.

In America, only a small minority seemed to have pronounced feeling on the question. Before he was fifty he had sent his "Mother," the most characteristically American painting he ever made, to the United States for exhibition and sale. But nobody purchased it—even for the five hundred dollars which the Pennells say he would have accepted—and it had to go back across the Atlantic and be sold to the French Government for a few thousand francs. Occasionally some recognition came to him from American artists. His champions wanted him to have more of it. He would have welcomed it himself. But an untoward fate always convinced him that he was not receiving it. He was constantly being reminded that his chief rôle was as a maker of *mots*. When friends tried to bring him forward in a serious rôle, complications seemed ready to develop from the most

WHISTLER AND AMERICA

trifling incidentals. Only a few months before his death, it was arranged that some of his pictures should be hung in an exhibition in New York. But Mr. Freer, the owner of them, and the hanging committee became so embroiled that one member of the committee was moved to resign, and Whistler was moved to write the letter—reprinted in the New York *Evening Post* and elsewhere—in which he expressed regret that his canvases had been "a cause of thought."

So he chose to end the chapter in England. He became an old man and sat in the sun. He was broken by the death of his wife—whom he had married late and who filled his life with a comfort he had never before known. He was sick at heart because he no longer had strength to do what he had at last learned to do without too much misgiving. One day the cables brought the news that he had died, at the age of sixty-nine. Impossible! He could not be old enough to die. Was he not still the unpredictable Jimmy? But two or three days later the cables brought the report of his funeral in the quiet little Chelsea church near which he had lived. Some of the dispatches played up the fact that the United States Embassy was not represented.

6

If only he had lived to be ninety and had made his long-deferred return then! If he could have stood for a moment on the eminence which his countrymen tardily assigned to him, and have taken a sweeping view of the scene, how unbelievable he would have found it! Not that he would have found in America any school of art that he had originated. But he was ferment. Wherever a picture of his appeared, there a healthy discussion began. In twenty years the ferment had time to work. University catalogues with scores of be-thumbed cards labeled, "Whistler, James (Abbott) McNeill!" A vast space in the Library of Congress set aside for the Pennells' priceless collection of Whistleriana! A gallery especially to house a collection of his paintings and etchings together with a priceless collection of the art of the Orient!

His Peacock Room carried away bodily from England and set up on a cold cement floor in the city of Washington! Clipping bureaus zealously filing every mention of his name! His "Ten O'Clock" reprinted in a popular magazine for general consumption! Prints of his "Mother" in countless living-rooms, in countless schoolhouses, and hanging above the wash basin or cookstove in countless obscure kitchens! The long forgotten house of his birth, saved from degradation, pointed out by the children in the street! An automobile tire company proclaiming that although James McNeill Whistler declared Russia to be the land of his birth, it is a pleasure to announce that he really was born in the city just eleven miles up the road—Lowell, Massachusetts!

If he could have seen all this, would not the Mephistopheles in him have sharpened the relish with which he looked?

"Ha! Ha! Have they gone in for Art? What!"

III

A Listener to the Winds

A LISTENER TO THE WINDS

I

EDWARD MACDOWELL meant to prove that there was a place for the serious musician in the United States of America. When he was fifteen he had gone with his mother to Paris and had studied for two years as a distinguished pupil in the National Conservatory; he had studied in Germany under Raff; he had taught in Germany and had married one of his American pupils; he had published compositions of interest; and from his German retreat he had looked out upon the world and drawn the conclusion that the place for him was back in his native country. Something of Walt Whitman's faith in democracy filled his spirit. There must be a place—a large place—for the artist in the United States. He meant to come home and occupy some part of this place himself, and reveal its possibilities to others.

2

For such an enterprise he possessed an interesting list of qualifications—a mere glimpse of the man would tell that. Far from being any long-haired, slender-fingered eulogist of moonbeams, he was a high-strung, energetic man for whom the whole business of existence was full of fascination. He was of more than average size—"the handsomest thoroughbred that ever stepped up to address a golf-ball"—and the mere spectacle of the world filled him with exhilaration. He tramped the hills of New Hampshire. He reconstructed for himself the life of the pioneers whose carefully wrought houses were now tumbling into the cellars or were being packed off piecemeal to New York to add a touch of distinction to interiors that needed it. He rode much with his farmer—sitting in the crowded seat of a high-wheeled sulky drawn by a brown, white-faced horse—and enjoyed the freshness of the farmer's philosophy. His wife, too, was blessed with an active mind, and whenever he was not at the moment away from the house, he was usually tagging along with her —in the garden, in the kitchen—to enjoy the spirited conversation. It was not unusual for this challenging woman and this energetic, blue-eyed, red-mustached but dark-haired Celt to sit in the light of the fireplace till one or two o'clock in the morning just to discuss books they had read, or theories of life they had thought of, or the prospects of the artistic-minded in America.

With the same eagerness he was forever exploring the world of books. He had never "enjoyed" a college education; no long mimeographed courses of prescribed reading had ever been delivered into his hands. Yet he was constantly finding excitement in books. Vitality was the thing! Aristophanes, Herodotus, Sophocles, Livy, Vasari's *Lives of the Painters,* Villari's *Life and Times of Machiavelli,* Schiller, Emerson, Tolstoy, Malory, Carlyle, Richard Jefferies, Fiona Macleod, the early writings of Woodrow Wilson—books of such variety he fed upon avidly.

As might be expected, the characteristics of this man were sharply marked. There were no ambiguous areas; he was very much one thing or very much another. He was, for instance, overwhelmingly creative-minded. The world he saw before him was not merely to be reflected upon; it was to be made into something new that he liked. So in addition to composing, he planned gardens, he designed buildings, he decorated rooms with comforting fitness, he made photographs—of the Alps, of New England—that were not less than works of art, he arranged furniture in harmonious combinations, and he made sketches with such skill that distinguished painters tried to induce him to turn to their art even after he had taken up music. On every new set of elements in the world, he felt an invitation to exercise the creative will, to enjoy the repose of deep concentration, to feel the warm blood in his pinkish face until he made something of the materials before him.

Likewise he was alertly scrupulous. Everything he did revealed his mental orderliness, his conscientiousness. Before the vogue of the typewriter and carbon copies, he kept letters received and his answers to them in a ledger-like notebook. On one page he pasted the letter addressed to him; on the page opposite he wrote a draft of his reply. This he interlined and compressed or expanded until he had a satisfactory version. Then he made the requisite copy on stationery. He wanted his accounts to balance to the penny, and went over the books of his farmer as an expert auditor might have done. He made his publishers change title-pages and dedicatory lines until every detail was perfect. When a friendly contemporary was about to publish an article on him and his work, but in a journal whose ethical code he could not approve, he demanded with cordial firmness that the article be sent to him at the rates paid by the publisher. "Purely business basis now."

His honesty often extended to great frankness and sometimes to amusing bluntness. Asked to join a national society of dignity, he replied: "In my opinion, ———'s speech last year was absolutely inexcusable, and the mere fact that such talk could be countenanced made me too doubtful of the society's good to join it." He thought Mark Twain overworked his high-priced methods of ridicule, and he did not hesitate to say so: "I shall make every effort to attend the dinner and only hope some committee will chloroform Mr. Clemens about speech-time. I fear his trying his hand on the Cervantes trick, and our chivalry is none too robust yet." And when an over-inquisitive woman appeared at Hillcrest, his summer home, and praised his modest retreat but asked critically why he had a field of corn so near the house, he answered without restraint: "Madam, that is so I may always be able to hide easily when I don't want to meet people who are coming to see me."

Such a frankly scrupulous person inevitably offends. A blunt letter to a man a thousand miles away who cannot see the sympathetic seriousness—or pleasant scorn—on the face of the writer will rarely prove agreeable. Yet when men came to know him, he was sought out precisely for his honest expression of opinion. "I do not find sufficient talent," he would write when he found none. Or if a dentist in the Mississippi Valley wrote that Paderewski had heard him play and had encouraged him to devote himself to the piano,

EDWARD MACDOWELL

MacDowell discussed the matter with such rightness, and pointed out with such friendly understanding the pitfalls in an art "where disappointments are too often the rule, not the exception," that the man could not fail to see his future with a new clarity. What could be the advantage of telling soft lies to people when doing so offends one's honesty and eventually causes somebody else infinite unhappiness?

His humor, too, stood in high relief. It was the robust element in the incongruous that delighted him. Up to a certain point he was serious —often very serious. Then at any moment he might break into a quiet chuckle or a very eloquent smile. Like most persons, he professed to be above puns; but when they became bad enough he always enjoyed them. Although at heart he really liked Brahms, he trained one of his dogs to bark with glee when he heard Wagner, but to howl dismally when he heard Brahms. He felt guilty, very guilty, when he once absented himself from a faculty meeting at Columbia University in order to see a prize fight; but he chuckled in great relief when he was able to discover, through the rifts in the tobacco smoke, that "about a third" of his academic colleagues were at the ringside with him. He was seriously disturbed when his farmer came to the house one day suffering from a great faintness in the region of the heart. Thinking that a spoonful of spirits might carry him through the crisis, he resorted to the family bottle of whisky. "Say when," he commanded, as he began to pour into a good-sized tumbler. But the farmer let him fill the glass and then hungrily tossed it off straight. At once MacDowell was in glee over the discovery of a heart too weak to perform ordinary duty, yet capable of withstanding unlimited shock!

His devotion, too, was so genuine, so impetuous, that it sometimes took on the character of the apostolic. Inhabitants of the village of Peterboro had no satisfactory golf-course. So he drew from the bank four-fifths of the money he had there, purchased a little farm that was for sale at a bargain price, presented it to the village, induced a generous-spirited neighbor to build a clubhouse, and invited everyone, even the humblest, to come and enjoy what he was pleased to call the royal game. Just as eagerly he gave himself to prospective musicians who possessed no money but gave evidence of ability and strong will. At times his free pupils were more numerous than those who were paying fees. And in an art notable for its jealousies, he was constantly extending to his less fortunate contemporaries—those whom he felt he understood—the cordial assurance of good feeling, the unmistakable evidence of regard. If one of his friends chanced to be putting on a new opera at the time he himself was about to hurry away from the city, why should not his trip be delayed? The mountains could wait; he just wanted to stay and see the thing through gloriously.

So, too, was he sensitive. With all of his impetuosity, if anyone should defer to him, he would bow and blush in embarrassment. And if there was prospect that his music might come up for consideration, he was ready to flee. When he could not escape hearing his compositions played poorly, his suffering could be paralleled only by that of

Joseph Conrad terrifyingly correcting some newly found errors in page proofs, or by that of Flaubert suffering so much over an imperfect passage in his prose, that he was for the moment ready to abandon all art. When he had himself played any of his compositions poorly, he would hide away—from his family, even—in darkest anguish. Often adverse criticism filled him with terror; at times even the contemplation of such criticism produced the same effect. "If the thing is a scorcher," he wrote to one of his intimates when an article by a young critic (who turned out to be wholly sympathetic) was about to appear, "I depend upon you for the tip, so that I can skip it when we return to town." So closely did the world come to him that the color of a forest, the temper of a wind, the clearness of a tone, or the brightness of a friendship was a matter of life and death.

3

Now it was this man who saw a place for the serious musician in America. He was not wholly unknown in his own country; his compositions had from time to time found their way over from Germany. But now he was eager to participate in American life more directly. So in 1888, when he was twenty-seven years old, he and his young wife took up their residence in Boston.

In a very short while he was participating in his new musical world with energy. He was soon known for his rather unconventional, impressionistic methods of teaching—"Make that run as if it were a sweep of color!" Soon too, he was busy with all sorts of musical adventures that exacted high ability and intent interest. Nor was it long before he was playing his own compositions with the Boston Symphony Orchestra, and giving independent recitals. He was a self-effacing person in his daily life, but when he undertook any task he worked with a pushing enthusiasm that could not fail to attract attention and command respect.

His recitals revealed much besides excellent playing. In preparation he worked furiously. "As I must play it next month,' he wrote to Teresa Carreño—who had always been an enthusiastic believer in his genius—"I am in a wild fury of mental and digital exercise." Just before the recital the "wild fury" terminated in a period of alternating flashes of doubt and eagerness, restless anticipation and stage fright. With few exceptions, his wife was with him just before he went upon the stage, and gave him the final push into his program.

In the presence of his audience, all his restlessness was fused in a powerful concentration upon his music, and he played not in the good form of the self-conscious artist, but in the engrossed, easy manner of one who is concerned with an idea and not a performance. This energetic man with the appearance of a thinker, and with good-sized, muscular hands, did not fill the specifications for a typical pianist. "He is a singularly unhinged and awkward-appearing person," said one of the Chicago newspapers in the earlier nineties, "and sways about upon his seat as if all the joints in his body had been freshly oiled. . . . He was repeatedly recalled, and nearly fell apart in bowing his acknowledgments."

After an hour and a half of this deep concentration and this generous responding to the enthusiastic acclaim of his listeners, he went from the concert hall more or less exhausted, to be sure, and often enough sick at heart because he felt that some detail of his work had been imperfect. He minimized the quality of his playing; he was not aspiring to be a pianist chiefly. Yet a casual leafing through of the newspaper comment upon his playing reveals more than one critic of national reputation giving support to the New York *Times* when it said: "He is the most satisfying pianist that has been heard here since Paderewski."

But with all of his success as a pianist, with all of his preoccupation with many matters, the composer in him was gradually emerging. As he came to be thought of as a composer, he became the center of the most lively discussion with which any American musician has thus far been honored. To-day when our spirits are accustomed to such virile, perplexing, yet withal reassuring productions as—let us say—Mr. John Alden Carpenter's *Skyscrapers,* it is extremely fashionable to refer to MacDowell as a very docile German romantic,

Yet in those days of his impetuous youth, he was hailed as a revolutionary. "MacDowell a Sensationalist—His Concerto Bristles with Innovations and Bizarre Effects," ran the headlines. "Wild, barbaric music," ran some of the comment. All in all, the great body of the comment was favorable. The newspapers recorded triumph after triumph for the composer in the principal cities of the country. Still, the character of his music had to be vehemently argued.

Ought he not to try for the great surging themes rather than silvery melodies and tone poems? Why does he persist in writing sonatas when everybody knows that the sonata has been consigned to perdition? Is it legitimate for the musician to express so much adoration for the out-of-doors? If he is going to employ classic forms, why does he take liberties with them? Isn't there something wrong with his music when he has to print a stanza of poetry at the top of the page in order to let people know what it is about? He is as much a realist as a romantic, and that is hardly a fair position for a romantic to take, is it? Why does he not compose more for the orchestra and less for the piano? Just what school does he belong to, anyhow? His music will not be permanent, will it?

Heaven knows, it is not for anyone to answer these questions, so much asked, so much argued. Some deserve no answer; some will be answered in due time. No one can say to-day, or to-morrow, whether his work will be permanent or not. The critics miss it just as badly as anyone else, and often worse. When no less a person than Dr. Johnson could believe that Blackmore's *Creation* was a poem that would transmit its author to posterity "among the first favorites of the English muse," and John Dennis thought that it infinitely surpassed Lucretius in certain respects, we should not be too glib in assigning people to their permanent places!

But when the eventual estimate of MacDowell is made, it will not disregard one fact: here was a poet, a Celtic poet, in the field of music—in the field of music in America. This fact illuminates many matters, if not all. It illuminates his love for folk-lore, his love for melody, his rebellious liberties with the classic forms, his devotion to suggestiveness, his own constant references to the poet in music, and his sharp feeling of the impossibility of a music strictly national. Above all, it makes clear the absurdity of classifying him. In strict literalness, he was the only one of his kind.

Only the young sculptor Bianchini has ever revealed MacDowell in the attitude of receptive listening. Yet that was the attitude characteristic of his mature life. The music of untold generations of his imaginative forbears sang in his ears. It was full of the shrieking north wind; it was full of the roaring sea; it was full of fairies and mysteries; it was full of sentiment not far removed—yet removed—from sentimentality; it was full of tragedy and of strange, unexpected quirks of humor. If only there were fewer lessons to give, fewer recitals and conferences; if only he could read and think and be receptive—he, a Celt living in the land of the American Indian, the Puritan, and an industrial civilization leavened a little by a degree of democracy—perhaps he might work it all out.

No man ever grew into a firmer conviction that

the great new life must somehow spring from the great old. "In my opinion, the crying need of our American students of music is not opportunities for study—but opportunities to get in touch with what was our world up to the last four hundred years." If one could know the past without being fettered by it in one's efforts to live in the present, new fundamental conceptions and new modes of expression might possibly be discovered.

In the course of his inquiries into the past, he became more and more certain that whatever spirit American music assimilated from Europe would be from the north rather than from the south. In this conviction his Celtic inclinations found logical encouragement. He read the mythology, the lore of the fireside, the poetry, the tales that satisfied his hunger. So greatly did he become interested in the writings of Fiona Macleod that he asked the privilege of dedicating his *"Keltic" Sonata* to him (to her, as he thought at the time it was) and only a misfortune to the letter of reply caused him after long waiting to dedicate the sonata to Grieg.

The spirit of these people whose blood coursed

in his veins cried to him to express in his peculiar way the life he found in the Western Hemisphere. He wanted to go to the brightest reaches, the most serene levels, the most austere depths. It was not any mere question of entertaining jaded people with a few novel sounds. "I will confess," he wrote to one of his intimates, "that I have moments in my work that make me believe in the supernatural. All this, however, is a precious thing, nor can I remember ever having spoken of it. My ideal I cannot even approach: if I really thought music a mere mixture of sound, or a vibratory means of affecting the body, I would never dream of wasting the poor rest of my life at it."

All of his youthful enthusiasm, all of his mastery of technique, all of the naturalness of power that comes only with mature years, converged in what might reasonably be expected to be the height of his genius. The way now seemed so much clearer to him that he wished some of his compositions that came from the foggy days of his early gropings had never been published. He talked more and more about the necessity of having composers with "poetic conceptions" if America were to produce any music.

Ironically enough, just when he was seeing his own way with greatest clarity, he was reminded that the public did not understand him. "Why, he declares that a poem is at the bottom of a piece of music," men and women said. "Then music is not an art in itself at all." Between a "poetic conception" and a piece of verse there was in their minds no difference whatever. And others said, "He has expressed a bully idea. Let's get together and organize things and have some American composers!" So they began to organize strictly American concerts. Precisely as though music composed in America was so scarce and so poor in quality that it could be guaranteed a hearing only when huddled together on a strictly American program! MacDowell explained that composers did not develop by such chamber-of-commerce methods—at first courteously, then bluntly, and later savagely.

If only the public possessed musical understanding! Here was something else for his ripening spirit to grapple with. He reflected much.

Every artist, he became convinced, especially if his work possesses either an audacious or a subtle originality, must sooner or later give a part of his time to interpreting himself and his class to the public—unless, of course, he prefers to remain misunderstood. Even Guy de Maupassant sometimes had to write prefaces! And especially was this creating of music so much of a mutual process in which the public must sustain the composer by coming up within his reach, that it was absurd to assume the patronizing attitude that the public might be disregarded or condemned. Mozart, Weismann had observed, would have had a hard enough time composing a symphony if he had been born in the Samoan Islands. If only one could get at this American public and bring up the level of its musical comprehension!

4

Just at the time MacDowell was giving thought to the musician's public, Columbia University established a professorship in music and invited him to accept it. The establishment of this professorship led to much discussion of what a university could or could not contribute to the music of a nation. Some persons doubted the wisdom of making musical instruction any part of a university's life. This argument was not new. In the early days before music was well established at Harvard, it is said that whenever the subject came up for discussion in a meeting of the Board of Overseers, Francis Parkman declared: "Musica delenda est." Now that the question was up at Columbia, there were all sorts of doubts about both music and universities. Mr. Theodore Thomas was quoted as saying: "When you have to entrust such a school to the management of men who know nothing about music, you run a great risk. In a university it would largely depend upon the attitude of the president toward music, and a change of presidents might seriously impair the work of the school." Others thought the instruction should be restricted rigidly to the teaching of "musical science and technique." Others thought the professor ought to hold the position merely as a comfortable means of enabling him to compose. And still others, perverted devotees of research, thought the work should be restricted to "searching the scientific principles upon which the instruments might be improved, the musical scale made more perfect, and the like!"

But MacDowell saw clearly what he thought ought to be done. Here was the coveted opportunity to remake the musical public. "My first wish was to bring music nearer to those who are to help make up our musical public of the future. The average well-educated man of to-day has but the vaguest idea of the aims of the poet in music. He absorbs his music through his ears alone." In his new position he would still have his long summer vacation for composing; and he could send out from his classroom a considerable body of men and women who would understand the function of the musician and give him a place among them when he chanced to appear.

He undertook his new duties with eager anticipations. The months of the academic year were crowded with counterpoint, instrumentation, symphonic forms, music drama, revolutionary influences, impressionism versus absolute music, the relation of music to the other arts; with conferences and letters of introduction and recommendation; with pianists who sought help in the making of their programs; with replies to ladies who had written—or found—verses which they hoped he would set to music; with interviews about prospective pupils whom parents saw bubbling over with genius; with criticisms of both composition and poetry submitted by young musicians; with the ordering of music and instruments for his department; and with class notebooks, examination papers, and reports to the university office. Then, late in May or early in June, he stole away from the city to his retreat in the hills of Peterboro.

Once there, he could "fuss around" with his farm until he was rested; then he could begin the season's work. In the pushing calm of the morning, he would slip off through the pine woods to his Log Cabin, and there work in the absolute quiet as long the music struggled for expression. Late in the day, if it happened to be one of those days when he had finished something, he carried the manuscript back to the house with him, and in the evening sat down at the piano in the music room to try it on his critic. Of her opinions he was more nervously expectant than of any other opinions in the world. Her feeling for his music was so sure that people with over-active tongues sometimes went so far as to say that she was the composer of some of it herself.

On one occasion when he was working on what he thought was a composition suggestive of a New England forest, he came home with the manuscript and held his customary evening tryout. When he had finished playing, his critic was silent. "Well?" he asked, half fearfully. "Oh," she replied, "I like it well enough, but that is not a New England forest; it is German." And so it was—an echo of years long gone. A perfect instance of the absurdity of trying to write strictly national music. So it had been an exceptionally good day, after all!

Despite the fullness of these earlier years at Columbia, they constituted the period of his most prolific and most important composing. Early in this period he produced his *Indian Suite,* about which James Huneker wrote: "At last we are treated to genuine American music, with roots plunged into aboriginal sources." Then followed the *Sea Pieces,* the *"Norse" Sonata,* the *"Keltic" Sonata,* the *New England Idyls,* the *Fireside Tales,* and numerous songs and choruses, including some for Columbia University. On these Columbia songs he worked so hard, he jocosely told President Seth Low, that his muse was "temporarily paralyzed by the continued strain of trying to find rhymes for 'Columbia' and 'Alma Mater'." Many of the things he had planned as a part of his twofold program he was now getting done.

Yet his experience at Columbia will always remain the perfect instance of the tragedy that overtakes creative genius when it casts its lot with any highly organized institution. He was sending out disciples to leaven the American public; and he was still finding time to do some important composing—and some less important. But he was wholly unblessed with the labor-saving instinct.

Before he came to the end of those precious years between thirty-five and forty-five, he had used up the energy that should have kept him productive until he was three score and ten.

And there were complications. Columbia elected a new president. Whether or not he belonged to the class Mr. Thomas had referred to as having a different attitude toward music, it must be said that after President Butler assumed control, Edward MacDowell was never comfortable. For a year he was on leave, and gave concerts with triumphal success in many parts of the country. When he returned to his academic duties—that is, in the autumn of 1903—he soon became convinced that comprehensive plans for further developing a new musical public through Columbia would be impossible—at least for him. He kept his disappointment within his own heart and meditated much upon it. What if all he had already done were futile? He was weary from many years of continuous exertion, and his great weariness provided an easy lodgment for this new fear.

At Christmas he and Mrs. MacDowell went to

New Hampshire for the vacation. There in the quiet of the snowy hills they reviewed the case and reached a decision. He would resign. His entire dream of remaking the American public through the ministrations of a great university seemed now as empty as Wagner's had seemed when he had sought to awaken the German public.

In this hour there was always one thought to cherish. He could compose. Why had he ever thought of doing anything else? He was only forty-three. What could not be done in twenty-five years? He meant to keep chiefly to the piano, to be sure. "The piano," he had written to a friend, "is a cold instrument, and a great thought written for it will exist as carven in stone when the ever-changing orchestral colors shall have faded —and they fade from year to year. . . . The piano, with all its wretched shortcomings, has reached a point of development where it will hardly change much more—has become permanent, so to speak— therefore I build my house on it." The piano, however, would leave time for other ventures in composition. He had conceived a kind of musical pantomime, a silent grand opera with only an accompaniment of music. And Mr. Henry T. Finck had long before said: "If he can get a worthy libretto, Mr. Edward A. MacDowell will write the first genuine American opera." So there were still some dreams to be realized!

But it is not so easy to disentangle oneself from a great university. When the news went abroad that he was resigning, may people wondered why. They wondered if there were not something to be cleared up. They were more mystified, too, because MacDowell's resignation came within a few days of that of Professor George E. Woodberry, although as a matter of fact, MacDowell had reached his decision quite independently. In reply to an article in the New York *Evening Post,* President Butler published a statement in which he declared that MacDowell was "a delightful colleague"; that his desire to devote all of his time to composition was his reason for resigning; and that the university had suggested to him that he accept a research professorship that would enable him to compose and at the same time retain his connections with Columbia—a plan that, President Butler said, MacDowell had taken under advisement. MacDowell, in order to correct this statement, sent to the *Evening Post* a copy of the letter that he submitted at the same time to the trustees of Columbia. It left no doubt about why he had resigned. He had been disappointed with what had been done in his absence the year before; he asserted that he had declined a nominal research professorship mentioned to him by President Butler because he was unwilling to associate his name with a policy he could not approve; and he reiterated that after putting his energy and enthusiasm into his work for seven years, he now recognized the futility of his efforts.

The trustees were deeply incensed that he should give out this information. In accepting his resignation, they incorporated in their letter a resolution of condemnation. "The Trustees," they said in closing, "regard Professor MacDowell's act in making public an official report, as an offense against propriety, a discourtesy to the Board, and a breach of that confidence which the Board always seeks to repose in every officer of the University."

To this MacDowell replied with clarity. "My letter to the Trustees," he said in part, "was a condensed repetition of a long conversation I had with President Butler. My aims and ideas he dismissed as being impossible and revolutionary. He, knowing all this, prints a plausible letter calculated to make the public think that my own work was my sole reason for leaving the University. My only means of righting this was an immediate protest. . . . As to my 'breach of that confidence which the Board always seeks to repose in every officer of the University,' I beg to say that the officers seek to repose this same trust in the members of the Board; and Mr. Butler's misleading communication to the press was a far graver breach of this confidence than my using the only means in my power to correct his statement."

Anyone in possession of the facts, MacDowell felt, would appreciate the fairness of his view of the case. But it is not always easy to possess "the facts." In such an incident, moreover, an impersonal institution has this advantage over an individual: it can become the hotbed of all sorts of deadly rumors that in the public mind take on the significance of facts, yet have no person within its organization who can be held responsible. "Some one has said"; "it is common report"; "it is generally understood"—and in a short while it is! Some of these rumors were to the effect that MacDowell had really done little teaching at Columbia; that academic duties were irksome to him; that he was incapable of systematic effort. All of these, some of which were eventually crystallized in the printed page, came to MacDowell's ears. To a sensitive man who had by dint of great labor, great sacrifice, and great good will developed a department from its foundation, they were unbearable. Always he had had little enough confidence in what he had done, but others had buoyed him up. Now these others—it so seemed to his tired mind—had suddenly begun to insist not only that he had done nothing, but that he had not tried. His nights became sleepless torture. Through all the hours—as the city lapsed into silence after midnight and became alive again before dawn—he went endlessly, frantically, hopelessly over the harrowing details. Where was there anything he might have done better? Always he came back to the conclusion that he had done his best—only to swing off again in the circle and go through the process once more. "This will kill me," he said one day, his face pallid and his mouth quivering.

Many of his students signed a petition asking him to reconsider his resignation. One class begged him to take them as private pupils the next year. At his last lecture the students presented him with a loving cup bearing an inscription of esteem and affection.

Finally when the episode seemed to be over, he turned to his composition. Here he was to encounter a still more terrifying futility. The busy years, finished off with an overwhelming disappointment, had left nothing at all. He was not only mentally weary, but mentally ill. Some thought, now that they stopped to reflect, that he had revealed signs of abnormality before. As a young man, it was pointed out, he had been crushed with grief and was morose over the sudden death of his beloved master Raff. A rumor made the rounds that for some time before he resigned it had been known up at Columbia that he was no longer sane. These opinions and rumors were at variance with the testimony of physicians who had known him intimately. They seemed to be at variance with the testimony of President Butler; for a university president does not ordinarily offer a research professorship to a man generally understood to be of unsound mind. They seemed to be at variance with the testimony of the trustees of Columbia; for usually a group of healthy men do not assail a mental invalid with a savage reprimand.

But about his illness now there could be no doubt. His friends and former colleagues were lost in pity when they looked upon this handsome body once quick with brilliance but now utterly without a mind. They wanted to do something helpful. Mr. Seth Low, former president of Columbia, went to MacDowell's wife and said: "I am partly responsible for this. Here is a check for five thousand dollars." A devoted young disciple made violin transcriptions of some of the more popular pianoforte compositions and turned over the resulting royalties. Heartening letters came from former colleagues, from former pupils, and from utter strangers. The affection which the musical public of America expressed for him at that time will always remain one of the encouraging proofs of goodness in the human spirit. He had reached more of the American people than he had ever believed—or now would ever have opportunity to believe.

His hair whitened. His face took on more and more the expression of one who looks but cannot comprehend. Sometimes the arrival of an old friend startled him for a moment into a pathetic effort at mental activity; sometimes it moved him to nothing more than a vacant stare. He sat in his easy chair by the window and looked vaguely away. He gazed at pictures in books of fairy tales as his wife turned the pages—the fairy tales that had once fascinated him and that were now among the last impressions to leave his mind. He fondled blankly the loving cup which had come to him from his students at Columbia. The months stretched emptily away and away. He drifted into absolute physical and mental helplessness. Then for months and months more he sat in abject silence —not the singing silence written about by one of his beneficiaries as the rightful heritage of the spendthrift poet in old age, but a dead gray silence too profound ever to be shaken by his own songs or those of any other.

IV

An Adventurer Out of the West

AN ADVENTURER OUT OF THE WEST

I

GEORGE BELLOWS'S short life was a joyous, unaccompanied pursuit. He looked about on the face of the earth and said: "Not so bad—as raw material. I wonder what it would all mean if you could get it straightened out so you could see it. And I wonder what it could be made to look like to anybody else." Before the bright terrestrial flash should pass he meant to explore as far as possible. There was not much to guide one. Why not inform oneself and act as one's own guide? Why not? He had all the capacities of a "lone wolf."

In trying to understand what he was about, his family, his friends, and the public were always a step or two behind; in trying to anticipate the direction of his next move, they were always wrong. His mother early dreamed that her slender, light-haired son would become a bishop. Every Sunday morning he was hauled to church in the high-wheeled surrey in the hope that his pushing young spirit would be impressed with the solemnity of mortal existence. Charley, a boy indentured by the family, had been so tremendously impressed that he decided to become an undertaker. In the back yard, in Columbus, Ohio, he fenced off a miniature cemetery and began with great enthusiasm to conduct funerals and inter remains. But George Bellows was interested only æsthetically: he made the designs for the tombstones that Charley erected. And as for the bishopric, the nearest he ever came to it was singing in a church choir—which is not necessarily a close approach. His father saw, evidently, that the bishopric was too far a reach. He proposed that his son become a banker. It would afford him an infinite peace in his last years to see this exploring son intrenched in an occupation of such solid respectability. But George said: "I don't want to be a banker. I'm going to Ohio State. I believe I can 'make' the baseball team."

In college he was a sprawling young barbarian

very much concerned with finding something to do. When he reported for baseball and the coaches and fans said, "He looks like an outfielder," he replied: "Oh, no; I'm a shortstop." And, despite the fact that shortstops are usually not six feet two inches tall, he went daily with a team-mate and practiced throwing to first base from every position on his side of the infield until he was accepted generally as the greatest shortstop that had ever played on an Ohio State team. He played basket-ball too, and he sang in the glee club. Still there was energy left. So when his fellows had played or sung until they were exhausted and begged for sleep, he devised ingenious means of keeping them awake. But still there was energy left. So he made cartoons of his professors.

The newspapers were full of comment on this boisterous, good-natured athlete. Fellow collegians and fellow townsmen said he was good enough for the big leagues. "Of course you will go into professional baseball." But he amazed them by replying: "Hu-uh! I'm going to be an artist."

"Whew!" was all they could say; and they said that under their breath.

It had never occurred to him that there might be any doubt about his qualifications as an artist. He had begun the fundamentals early. In the rigid Methodist days of his childhood he had been permitted two activities on Sunday—reading and drawing. Since his mother always delighted in reading to him, he could draw undisturbed while he listened! That meant that he drew all the time on Sunday afternoons. This experience—and he always thought it had much to do in determining his career—enabled him to draw better than any of his fellow pupils in school. He was known as "the artist." In college he illustrated undergraduate publications. Professor "Joey" Taylor, sympathetic confessor for all brave spirits at Ohio State, encouraged him to believe that his ability was important. But in New York he encountered people who were not so sure. He came from way out in Columbus, Ohio, did he not, or some other unheard-of place? What did anybody know about art out there?

He met one teacher, however, who immediately supported his confidence in himself—Robert Henri. Henri had come from the Middle West himself, and he liked this stalwart chap with the intent face and the healthy will. A pupil who was always gay, always full of deviltry, yet always serious about the business of painting, was not to be found in the New York School of Art every day. From every word his original-minded teacher uttered, from every movement he made, from every criticism he offered, Bellows learned with white-hot mind. Henri never criticized anyone else so severely. He knew Bellows could stand what would crush others. But he also encouraged him. "You will succeed," he assured him; "some degree of success is certain. The quality of your success will depend upon the personal development you make." So, after all, maybe he might paint just as good a picture as anybody!

His fellow students looked upon him with inquiring, amused eyes. He was so little acquainted with the life of New York that the only social organization he knew when he arrived was the

Y.M.C.A. It maintained a swimming-pool and a basket-ball floor, and he knew how to use both. In appearance nothing marked him as a devotee of the æsthetic. He was self-conscious in the presence of so many artistic strangers; he sprawled—there was so much of him that it was difficult to be graceful except when standing up; and he laughed with such untrammeled heartiness that everyone turned and stared at him whenever anything set him going. But how much did he care? Perhaps, if he only knew the truth, they were all just as raw as he was. Maybe they didn't know half as much about painting! Certainly they didn't know one-tenth as much about it as he meant to know some day.

No one could deny that he was interesting. His fellow students soon became busy in trying to make him out. His clumsy externals could not prevent them from seeing his essential good nature, his essential dignity of spirit, and his sound emotional and intellectual power. They liked especially his glowing vigor. When the school had its first dance of the year he took a very beautiful Scandinavian girl—from Minnesota. His friends stood in wonder at the magnificence of this light-haired couple. "Wouldn't they make a prize-winning bride and groom?" everyone asked. But when the whisperings came to Bellows he exclaimed: "Oh, no! You are absolutely wrong! I'm going to marry that dark-haired girl from Upper Montclair!"

This girl from Upper Montclair, Miss Emma Louise Story, out of sheer pity for an overgrown boy who was spending his long Christmas vacation away from home, invited him to come to her father's house for a meal. "The steak," she assured her mother, "must be the biggest one you can find; for I never saw such an eater as he is." But George was so nervous he could not handle the silverware, much less eat. His embarrassment was increased, too, by the young lady's father. He did not care much for male artists. He had known one, a man who could paint a feather so perfectly that you couldn't tell it from the real thing; but, apart from being able to do that, he did not count for much. This feeling against artists was accentuated, too, when George Bellows began to appear on the landscape with a degree of regularity. But George was ready to contest with the father as well as with the hesitant daughter. What does a little matter of waiting around for six years amount to?

All the while he was painting, painting with unequaled persistence. "No time to waste! No time to waste!" One day John W. Alexander went home from his duties as a juror in the National Academy's annual exhibit and said to his wife: "There's a picture over there, by a young fellow named Bellows, from out West somewhere—'Forty-Two Kids' he calls it—that you must see. There's genius in it." Others saw it and were startled. "But," some of them asked, "is it an artistic subject? Do such things as boys in swimming lend themselves to artistic treatment?" "Why not?" Bellows asked in reply, and went on painting. He painted the river front, the prize-ring, the crowd in the steaming street, the city cliff-dwellers, the circus, the stevedores on the docks. All the things possessing everyday dignity and significance but long treated with disdain, all the unglorified

GEORGE BELLOWS

Photograph by Nicholas Haz

struggle of his kind, cried to him for expression. The uncomprehending dismissed it as wild art, decadent art, drab art! They declared that Billy Sunday had broken into the æsthetic world. Those who were more sympathetic said: "Now we are getting him. He believes in painting the red-blooded American life. He is the painter with the punch!"

So he was hailed as the artist who made things anybody would understand; so, too, was he as completely misunderstood as ever. For if he was the painter of the vigorous, the physically dramatic, he was to be even more the painter of the subtle and the intimate. If he could produce "Sharkey's," he could also produce "Spring, Gramercy Park"; "Blue Snow, the Battery"; "Crehaven"; "Aunt Fanny"; "Portrait of My Mother"; "Emma in Purple Dress"; "Anne in White"; "Lady Jean"; "Portrait of Katherine Rosen"; "Eleanor, Jean, and Anna."

His diversity had kept the public guessing, yet he did not find enough in the entire range of painting to keep his own mind busy. It is not so easy to paint in New York in the dead of winter. Inasmuch as he liked black and white and enjoyed working on stone, he took up lithography. "But what are you doing that for?" his admirers asked. "Who cares anything about lithography in these days? If you want to work in black and white you ought to etch."

"But I can't etch," he insisted, "and I can make lithographs."

"But don't you wish to sell your work?" dealers protested. "There is no demand for lithographs."

"Then," he replied with characteristic braggadocio, "we'll put lithographs on the map!"

And he did. The first prints attracted favorable attention. One of his intimates counseled him: "You had better slip one or two proofs of each stone away and keep them a while. The price might go up; you might make some money." He took the advice and he and his wife had much amusement over the fund they were going to develop for the college education of Anne and Jean. They never dreamed that the day would come when some of these prints would sell for a thousand or twelve hundred dollars apiece.

In lithography he found just the right opportunity to round out his record of America's emotional life. The stone served perfectly for many brief chapters that did not readily admit of treatment in color: "Village Prayer-Meeting"; "Initiation in the Frat"; "Benediction in Georgia"; "The Shower-Bath"; "Dance in a Mad-House"; "Old Billiard-Player"; "The Law Is Too Slow"; "Billy Sunday"; "Sixteen East Gay Street"; "Dempsey and Firpo"; "Business Men's Class, Y.M.C.A."; "Electrocution." In lithography, too, he could laugh as much as he liked. His "Reducing," the representation of a meek-looking husband calmly asleep in bed, and his very stout wife flat on her back on the floor doing some very energetic exercises, will be amusing as long as there are fat women of social importance in the world. A very stout woman, one day after Bellows had become somewhat the vogue among those who interest themselves in art socially, entered a museum and asked what there was new to be seen. She was told that yonder was a new lithograph by George Bellows. "Oh, how lovely!" she exclaimed, bringing her lorgnette to bear upon it as she moved nearer. "What is it, a shell?" When she saw, she was scandalized, and turned away with disgust that could be expressed only in a violent crescendo of "Pooh! Pooh!! Pooh!!!"

"Now we have him at last," the public said, after his lithographs had become current. "He gives us life just as he sees it. He has ability—great ability perhaps—but he lacks the imagination to make anything wholly new from simple elements. He cannot express himself in the symbolic." Then he produced "Edith Cavell," and later "Allan Donn Puts to Sea"; "The Return to Life"; "Amour"; "Punchinello in the House of Death"; and "The Crucifixion." In truth, he began to reveal so much interest in such subjects that some of his contemporaries were disturbed. Joseph Pennell, known for his ability in combat as well as for his ability as an artist, on one occasion at the National Arts Club enlarged upon the dangers of painting when one has not the object before one at the time.

"George Bellows," he went on to say, "would have made a better painting of Edith Cavell if he had been on the spot and seen with his own eyes. He was not there, certainly." When he had finished, Bellows was asked to discuss the point. In proceeding he said: "No, I was not present at the execution of Edith Cavell. I had just as good a chance to get a ticket as Leonardo had to get one for the Last Supper!"

2

When a man of such capacity to go his own way emerges from surroundings where he might little be expected to appear, he soon becomes a legend. Everybody wants to know about him. Few had learned about the personal George Bellows. He had not been seen much either in high places or in Bohemia; he had been too busy. But when people did see him, unless they came to know him intimately, they were as much mystified as ever. He did not conform to their notions of a great artist. He was only one of those typical Americans whom

Americans are always talking about but rarely see. When they do see one, they have difficulty in believing their own eyes; he seems too good to be true.

Most of those magnified American qualities whose names have been outworn, but whose essences have not, he possessed. For instance, he was full of the American's gusto. He was unafraid to like things. Wherever he went everything was interesting and moving. Life was full of emotions to which he would give organized expression, architectonic integrity. The spectacle of New York—the Hudson, the East Side, the Battery, the parks—filled him with such enthusiasm that he confessed great difficulty in stopping long enough to paint what he saw. Columbus, Ohio, was just as interesting; people back there were bully, even if he did sometimes laugh in their faces. The spectacle that men make for themselves was fascinating, too. When he went to the theater—and he went often—he laughed with such unrestrained and honest joy that he heartened not only the audience but the actors. "Can't you see anything interesting?" he asked somewhat impatiently. The soporific "pure art" that the disillusioned and the burnt-out produce in an effort to "escape" something or other did not concern him. His times were overwhelming in their possibilities. He had fun in finding what seemed most significant, and he had greater, agonizing fun in struggling to expression. When one of his most brilliant portraits had been placed on exhibition with a note in the catalogue implying that it had been painted as a commission, he corrected the error by writing: "Painted for fun." He liked the world. He liked his friends. He liked himself pretty well, thank you, and his own work. And he liked good work done by others. No one ever joined the procession of honor with more enthusiasm than he did when he discovered genius in the work of somebody else.

American, too, was his zeal as a crusader. He was always fighting for causes. "I am a patriot for beauty. I would enlist in an army to make the world more beautiful. I would go to war for an ideal—far more easily than I could for a country." *The Masses,* a journal which Bellows had hoped might do something for the people to whom it was addressed, slowly deteriorated, and he drew up a complete program for its rejuvenation—and supported his contentions vigorously. Convinced that the jury system employed by the National Academy for selecting pictures for the annual exhibit was unfair to the young variants who did work of marked individuality, he waged war—a long and hot war—against the majority system of selection. "The iconoclasts among us, and I count myself one," had many changes to propose that would give the unlabeled man a better chance to have his work seen. And he was interested in international good will. Despite the fact that from the beginning to the end of his life he never left his own shores to visit another country, he dreamed of universal friendship. Especially did he wish to have his own country and France understand each other. One of the great enthusiasms of his life was the promotion of an American exhibition for the Luxembourg at the time of the World War.

There were, too, less agreeable matters that called for the crusader. The editor of an art journal undertook to have artists pay for his news notes about them and for the space that he proposed to devote to reproductions of their work. George Bellows wrote to the editor that he had always supposed news notes and reproductions were published because they were of public interest, and not because they were paid for as advertising. He would not lend himself to any such graft. The editor attempted to justify himself by saying that since every artist would buy space, there would be in the end a right comparative representation. Bellows asked what was going to happen to the good artist who chanced not to have money with which to buy news about himself, and proceeded to wage the most extensive war possible upon the editor and his practices. There was always something to fight for —or against!

He had the crusader's faith, too. Things might be bad enough—he sometimes declared that conditions were "rotten"—but they could be made better. "It is not because America has great wealth, great opportunities," he said, "and what is blandly termed 'great educational facilities' that she has any claim to the attention of the world's culture.

It must some day be because of the fact that, among the vast sum of her population, there appears now and then a man who can create things of wonder and beauty." To this end something might be done. He did not, he protested, expect Mayor Hylan to proclaim a holiday when Glackens produced such a masterpiece as his "Portrait of Walter Hampden." Yet why should not an artist's neighbors in general be led to see their own need of art with such burning clearness that they would be moved to provide the artist with a normal, legitimate economic support? "A great artist," he was accustomed to say, "can exist in a country which buys bad art; his situation is more difficult in a country which buys none." Nor need the public fear to buy the work of American artists. When the citizens of our own country free themselves from traditional prejudices and are able to exercise their own sense of delight, their own judgment, they will see how distinguished much American painting is. "It is not necessarily ridiculous to have faith. It is, however, very important to have it. Among some of our artists some time the great genius of America will arise. Some of him is probably here now. Look!"

American also was his feeling that he was just as good as the other fellow—at least. He never felt inferior; in fact, he liked the center of the stage. He was a brother to a certain manner of American soldier, who boasts before a battle that he will do thus and so, and then makes good his boast. He was not awed by sophistication; he could always match it with homely wisdom. He would pit himself against the most skillful, the most argumentative, and enjoy the experience. From the Catskills he wrote: "I have called it a summer, taken stock, showed the work to everybody, and am ready to pack up, go to New York, and start arguing with Pennell." And his feeling of equality or better he maintained in the presence of the most experienced, most "authoritative" art critics. Instead of waging a defensive war, as Whistler so often did, or suffering unspeakable agony, as Edward MacDowell did when assailed by the unintelligent, Bellows smoked the matter over a little, took his sturdy pen in hand, invited the critic to draw and paint a while in order to discover how much he did not know, and told him to go to hell. "So that's that. I've got to paint."

In keeping with the great American legend, too, he was a family man. He gave the best of himself—his ability, his good humor, his boyish fun, his profound affection—to his kin. His father, an "Amen Methodist," was fifty-five years old when George was born. He was unapproachable on many matters close to a boy's heart. Yet George loved him while he stood in awe of him. "By charging less than he was worth," he once wrote of his father, an architect and builder, "and by investing in worthy causes, his fortune remained reasonably easy to calculate. He planned for me to become president of a bank. He had, however, the greatest respect for Michael Angelo, holding him second to no man with the exception of Moses. His main feeling seemed to be sorrow for the hard life I would be forced to lead as an artist in this generation. In this, owing greatly to his own support, he guessed wrong."

With this father it was not easy to be whimsical.

But he could be with his mother. With her he could play the clown and the tease as much as he liked. He never ceased to chide her about his poor bringing-up, to make pseudo-sacrilegious remarks about the things she held sacred, to enlarge upon her son's financial plight, or to be shocked by the great range of vices that her Methodism permitted.

"Dear Ma:
'The melancholy days are come,
The saddest of the year,
When the sluice gates of the pocketbook
Are opened from the rear.'"

Or:

"And what is the name of the new pastor?
"And does he Chew?
"Now, now, now, don't be angry. Don't you remember Dr. Smith?
"Have you been flinching from Dominoes or dominoing from Flinch?
"Answer yes or no."

And who ever had such a wife and such daughters? Emma, whom he had won after six years of the most studious persistence! With all of his uproarious nonsense, he could never be wholly nonsensical about Emma. He loved her too passionately, too profoundly. And there were "the kids— Anne the slim and Jean the bean." He romped with them; he devised and wore the most astounding costumes to startle and delight them; he gave them the liberty of the studio while he worked; he wrote them letters in verse—good enough to be published; he dreamed of them; and he painted them in the best pictures he ever made.

And when the lean years were over and he seemed to have a long stretch of full ones ahead, he began to express his affection for his kin in new ways. To Aunt Fanny—the Aunt Fanny of the portrait, and the Eleanor of the "Eleanor, Jean and Anna"—he always felt especially attracted. She had helped to look after him when he was very small, and had kept him immaculately combed up and clean; and she had experienced the great romance of refusing twice to marry the man who loved her, and then accepting him the third time! But her possessions were few and her pride great. So when he once invited her to come to the Catskills for a visit, and received no reply, he suspected the reason. In the course of a shrewdly tactful letter, he wrote:

"I am aware, my dear Aunt Fanny, that you have not been blessed with the best of luck. I have. Therefore, I think it would be a nice idea to try and strike something like a mean proportion.

"I have what I think is a well-grounded belief that both you and your daughter Laura would welcome a vacation from the same scene—if you are anything like me. I must change around a bit.

"Further than this, I want to feel that you are not needing to worry about the future. As the chances are that it would not be a very available plan to leave you something in my will, I think I will leave you something right away. My mother is going to do exactly what I am proposing for myself, and between us you are to have a regular income of a thousand a year, which added to what income you have of your own, should make the days comfortable."

Then, after a description of his country place, and the information that the round-trip tickets and money for incidentals were on the way, he added the clinching postcript that he had chosen his picture of her to represent him in "the great exhibition in the Luxembourg, Paris."

He met the requirements of the national legend, finally, by combining a homely exterior with an essential refinement. He was tall, he was ungainly in some of his movements, and early he became bald. In addition, he was a believer in the informal. As a result, he looked much of the time like a plumber. Always he was making something at his work-bench on the mezzanine floor of his studio. He must have at hand every conceivable kind of nail and screw and bolt. For these he went to a neighboring hardware-store, where the salesmen liked him so much that they proudly kept the newspaper reproductions of pictures made by this customer who knew the names and sizes of nails as if he might be a person of solid character. In the country he plunged into every kind of manual labor. When his new house was ready for the roof he went to work on it. "Why don't you hire a man to do it?" his wife protested. "Can't ask anybody else to do what I'm afraid to do myself." But sitting on an unroofed house in the summer sun is not the easiest of chores. His untoughened body became so sore that he could scarcely proceed. But he stuffed a pillow into his overalls and worked valiantly, painfully on, until he had driven the last nail in the last shingle.

In general, strangers gained the impression that he was uncouth. When he was not sprawling, he was rocking. He brought from the Middle West the rocking-chair state of mind. So, whenever there was nothing else to do, he rocked—energetically, obliviously. Sometimes one of his intimates, who confessed that he loved the man more than a brother, would command: "You stop that rocking!" He would stop for a time. But as soon as the conversation or the meditation became absorbing again he fell into his rolling, swaying pace.

Yet in all matters of the spirit he was one of the most sensitive of men. He could not endure any music short of the best; he refused to listen to it even when played by Emma! He read not only great books, but books which require unusual refinement of intellect and feeling in the reader. Plays, too, must have quality. And his friends had to come up to the same requirements as his plays and books and music. When some one criticized him for having only friends of intellectual or artistic brilliance, he retorted: "What do you suppose I have friends for—to be bored by them?" His handwriting was that of a crude country boy, and he did not always spell according to the dictionary; yet he possessed a startling sense of fitness in words, a feeling for the rhythmical power in a sentence, and a perfect intuition for the total effect that a paragraph or a letter would produce.

3

Now a man with such an array of traditional American qualities would excite wonder—if not skepticism—wherever he chanced to appear. But the wonder was almost inexpressibly great when he chanced to appear in the world of art. Questioned concerning the peculiar artistic circumstances in which he arose, he replied jovially: "I arose surrounded by Methodists and Republicans!" And what he humorously implied was literally true: almost everything surrounding his early life, viewed in the obvious manner, was non-artistic.

Yet it is just because his individuality came from such an environment that he was able to make his greatest contribution to art. The tendency of art when it is wholly in the hands of organizations devoted to its perpetuation is to become ascetic, overrefined, "arty." American art schools for some decades have been filled, in the main, with young ladies who develop a technique for doing nothing in particular with great skill. If art is not to become drivel, there must constantly be injected into it some of the life of the soil, something that corresponds to the uncultivated health of a robust body. It requires a cross-fertilization of sanity from "the provinces." Somebody must occasionally give to it a strain of life comparable to what Abraham Lincoln gave to politics.

It was this fresh life, this instinctive feeling for a healthy relation, that Bellows brought to art. He was unalterably a lone wolf. If somebody who professed to be very wise said in patronizing fashion, "Now, that is the way artists do that," Bellows was certain to reply: "Well, hold on! Let's take a look. I don't know whether it is or not!" Not that he had any closed system of his own! "He was the readiest man in the world to have you prove that you were right," said the person who was the greatest single influence in his life as a painter; "but you had to prove it. He always brought himself to his work." This habit of bringing himself to his work was what led many to call him a revolutionist. "If I am," he said, "I don't know it. First of all, I am a painter, and a painter gets hold of life—gets hold of something real, of many real things. That makes him think, and if he thinks out loud he is called a revolutionist. I guess that is about the size of the matter." The reasonable thing to do, he contended, was to "watch all good art and accept none as a standard for yourself. Think with all the world and work alone."

Many, in attempting to evaluate his contribution, have compared him with Kipling, with Jack London, with Whitman. In each comparison there is a certain soundness. But he had more warmth, more fluidity, than Kipling; and he was more comprehensive in his sympathies, more healthy in his vigor, than Jack London. The parallel with Whitman is closest. Both were impatient with outworn forms and outworn subjects; both felt the energy of American life and were able to express it; both believed in the sacredness of the individual and hesitated not to take pride in themselves; and both believed that the artist should celebrate all life, whether "beautiful" or not, that reveals significance.

But Bellows was a more complete person than Whitman, a more representative person. Whitman was, with all of his democracy, an exotic democrat. He was an exotic American. He was not himself representative; he only wrote about representative things. He was, moreover, in his sympathies a remote pagan, and George Bellows was close and warm and reverential. Bellows might easily have painted something comparable to "The City Dead House," "By the Bivouac's Fitful Flame," "O Captain, My Captain," or "With Husky Haughty Lips, O Sea," but if Whitman had tried for a lifetime, he never would have written anything having the emotional tone of "Aunt Fanny," "Emma and Her Children," or "Lady Jean."

But any attempt to compare Bellows with somebody else must always be for convenience of discussion merely. The comparisons always turn out to be contrasts. He was made in his own proportions of vigor, understanding, dramatic power, humor, intimacy; and he had his own methods of supplanting the malarial sentimentality of American art with a robust sentiment.

4

Nothing in anybody's effort to "place" him in the world of art, nothing in the solid fame that yearly became more solid, ever lured him away from the great pursuit. He meant to attain a perfection that Columbus, Ohio, and New York City had little dreamed about. He wanted to learn just because he wanted to learn. He was ready, too, to learn from anybody—from the ancient masters, from the most youthful of his artistic contemporaries, from the philosopher, from the fool. If he discovered some day that he was securing an effect as Tintoretto had secured it, he must write to his friends about the whole matter with boyish delight. If a new exhibition, a new school, or a new process was announced, he had to look into it at once to see if there were not something to learn. Such a possibility he approached with sublime expectancy. After he had gone through a new exhibition with alertness, he would say, "Nothing here I have not already learned"; or, "I mean to work until I can finish a canvas as perfectly as that myself." He was enthusiastic over the appearance of Jay Hambidge's *Dynamic Symmetry,* and later made frequent acknowledgment of his indebtedness to the volume. He was just as enthusiastic over new possibilities in color. If he applied himself to his painting until he grew stale and was unable to make progress, he did not try to sink into a restful stupor, but went to Brentano's, bought an armload of good solid reading, and buried himself from the world until he felt restored. "Can't paint if I don't feed my mind!"

By the time he had carried on his pursuit until he was forty, he had become the enriched person that must go into the making of a great artist. He was a philosopher, wise in his own increasing humility. "Try it in every possible way," he once told some art students. "Be deliberate—and spontaneous. Be thoughtful and painstaking. Be abandoned and impulsive. Learn your own possibilities. There is no impetus I have not followed, no method of technique I am unwilling to try. There is nothing I do not want to know that has to do with life or art." He was no longer—if he ever had been—a good-natured barbarian who had hit upon good painting and good lithography, but a man who had some coherent notions of the ways of men and artists. "Art isn't made in Bohemia, neither is it not made in Bohemia. It is wherever life exists and expresses dignity, humor, humanity, kindness, order." He quoted with approbation the words of Robert Henri: "To hold the spirit of greatness is in my mind what the world was created for—and art is great as it translates and embodies that spirit."

More and more he became impatient of mere formalities. "The Independent show this year is a hummer," he wrote in a letter. "The only stalling was on this damned dance which none of us want to go to. *And will not!*" What he wanted was a day that would give him a chance to work his head off, sometimes on a new canvas, often enough on one that he had kept about for months or years. In 1920 he wrote to a friend: "Have three fine portraits of Anne, Jean, and Emma, with no heads on any." Three years later the satisfying head was still not on Emma. After repeated attempts at it, he had her sit for him again one morning in the country. "Can't do it! Give it up! Go on!" he cried. But before she got away he called: "Come back here! Let me try just once more!" And in an hour the head that has been so widely praised for just the right reflective attitude was completed.

When he had worked himself to exhaustion he would call up one of his friends: "Hello! Is this Frans Hals?"

"Why, yes, Michael Angelo!"

"Well, how about a game of pool?" Or, if possible, baseball or tennis; he was not enough of a loafer to master pool.

Then dinner and music, or the theater, or some hours over a new lithograph, if he chanced to be in the city. Sometimes he worked on his lithographs till two in the morning, up on the mezzanine floor of his studio. That was the life!

There was ever a little crusading to do, too. Less than a year before the brief, agonizing days in the hospital that brought all to an end, the editor of a journal cut shamefully an illustration that Bellows had made under contract. "Result," he wrote, "the most awful botch imaginable. Emma has ordered me to war. I have gone. After two letters, very well done, not a glimmer of guilt from the editor. So I have started a legal attack—I expect to lose money, but I hope to line up the art world and get some kind of protection against the arbitrary changing of artists' work."

But nothing could permanently ruffle him. He was still the boisterous adventurer. The night before he was stricken with appendicitis—and he was only forty-two—Robert Henri had a number of friends in for the evening. They were the group that Bellows called "The Society of Perfect Wives and Husbands." As usual, he was much in the center of the stage. He found some old clothes and made himself up as Queen Victoria. Either because his friends were in special need of amusement or because he was in very high spirits, he never seemed such a perfect clown. The evening lasted until one or two o'clock. When the guests departed they descended from the studio—on the third floor—together. In the quiet that followed, the host stood by the window looking reflectively out. Below in the street there was a burst of laughter—genuine, honest, infectious laughter. It was George Bellows moving off into the night.

V

A Self-Indulgent Apostle

A SELF-INDULGENT APOSTLE

I

For his own peace of spirit, Charles Eliot Norton saw the earth at an unfortunate time. He was destined to love everything that was beautiful and to hate everything that was ugly. Yet where did the fates spread his life if not so that his best years fell in the latter part of the nineteenth century? As a child, as a youth, as a man of early middle life, he had opportunity to develop natural alertness into a sensitiveness almost unparalleled. And then he was to be surrounded in his maturer years by "President Grant" architecture, an August-afternoon listlessness in American letters, degeneracy in politics, and roughshod, deforming methods in industry.

Suppose he had lived a quarter of a century earlier! Suppose the struggle over slavery had come in his middle sixties so that he might have felt—along with many another elderly man—that he was rounding out his little cycle to glorious completion by winning a war! It is conceivable that he might then have been content to fill the rôle of conversationalist, and smoke away the pleasant last years in the company of Lowell and Longfellow, chatting over the great poems of the past, and the somewhat less great poems of the immediate hour. It is conceivable that his lot might have fallen in such a languorous time that he would have been lulled into one of the dreamiest of the lotus-eaters. For in his nature the inclination to be self-indulgent and the inclination to be apostolic were so nicely balanced that the accidents of environment were enough to push the one ahead of the other.

As it turned out, his life became an unceasing contest between these two inclinations. The lover of the plenteous got an early start. At twenty-two he had gone to India—as a young business man—and was sipping tea with the Royal Poet of Delhi, Maha Rajah Apurva Krishna Bahadoor. These were rapturous hours for the glowing youth. And there were other rapturous hours. He enjoyed some of them in the Egyptian desert. He enjoyed others in Venice. He enjoyed others in Paris. In Paris he sat proudly on the stage at a benefit where the incomparable Rachel recited scenes from *Virginie,* and he almost touched her hand as he dropped his gold piece into the velvet bag she passed among the guests. In Paris he went with Count Circourt to spend an evening—as it turned out, a pretty dull one—with Lamartine. And he enjoyed still other of these rapturous hours in Florence. What young man just out of college might not be pardoned for enthusiasm in his letters after sitting intimately with the Brownings in the evening quiet of their own Italian house?

The apostolic in him had its opportunities, too. He grew up in a period of American history when helping men to aspire was regarded as a high kind of activity. In Boston he observed how poorly workingmen were housed. While these conditions existed he could not remain self-indulgently at ease. He talked with older men—this quiet, somewhat radiant young gentleman—about Model

Houses and their social importance. He succeeded in having Model Houses built. He talked about the success of the venture—and eventually wrote about it—with such conviction that his dream was taken up in other cities. Extraordinary place for a building reform to originate—in the heart of a young man so largely occupied by the Royal Poet of Delhi, Rachel, and the Brownings! But it was an extraordinary heart.

Still these years were full of pleasant self-indulgence. The voice of Abraham Lincoln crying out to the people of Illinois that the slavery question was more than a question of economics did not penetrate the woodland of Shady Hill in Cambridge, Massachusetts. Here he entertained Arthur Hugh Clough; he lighted innumerable good cigars with Longfellow and Lowell and the rest of his friends. He whiled away long summer months "in lounging and reading and writing." He witnessed the advent of Walt Whitman, who seemed to him to combine "the characteristics of a Concord philosopher with those of a New York fireman." He witnessed the advent of Darwin and the consternation he brought not only to the orthodox of the church but to the orthodox of the scientific world. In Charleston he learned how the people of the South combined bounteousness and good taste. In Rome he smiled up to Mrs. Gaskell from the Italian crowd, and carried bouquets to her devotedly. Back in England, he enjoyed the buoyancy of Clough again, and the dogmatic sagacities of Ruskin.

But he could not permanently escape interest in the slavery question. The voice of Abraham Lincoln on the plains of Illinois did eventually echo through his Cambridge woodland. His mind was prepared: he had thought much about social life —though it must be said, in pretty conservative fashion. Slavery, he came to believe, had nothing in it that was not evil. For the slave-holders he had a feeling of magnanimous pity. The institution was more deadly to them than to the slaves. He did not approve John Brown's methods, but he did approve his high desire to arouse the people. Slavery was plunging the whole country toward ruin, and many people of the North were indifferent to what was going on.

He was frail of body. But when the war came he gave himself with fervor to such work as he could do. At first he doubted Lincoln. Why did the people choose him instead of Seward for the presidency? But the war must go on even if the President did chance to be infirm in character and in language! Public opinion, almost hopelessly unstable in parts of the North, must be stiffened up. Through the Loyal Publication Society—a forerunner of the newspaper syndicate—he and some friends distributed encouraging broadsides to newspaper editors throughout the North. The cause for which he worked was as high, he believed, as men had ever fought for. He must give it support in every way within his modest power.

Once a man gets into a fight, he discovers how interesting a fight may be. He had had the experience of helping to found the *Atlantic Monthly;* and now he became one of the editors (with James Russell Lowell) of the *North American Review.*

Here he had larger opportunity to speak for his country. He enjoyed the experience. He was proud of what he was able to do. But the more he gave himself to the enterprise the more he became convinced that such a magazine as the *Review* was insufficient as a journal of opinion. There ought to be some journal published every week; the pressure on public opinion ought to be constant. So just as the war was coming to an end he helped to found the *Nation*—and he was proud of that job, too.

Then he had to give attention to the wrong-headedness of his British friends. Why should they persist in looking upon the North with disfavor? Ruskin, for example, professed to be performing scout duty for the entire human race; yet he failed even to understand what was going on west of the Atlantic. "The war," he declared, "has put a gulf between all Americans and me so that I do not care to hear what they think or tell them what I think on any matter." Norton's position required both gallantry and fortitude. He never forgot that his correspondents were his friends. But he never failed to let them understand his loyalty to his country's ideal.

He had become engrossed in enterprises. Yet just when the war was out of the way, just when the first two or three years after the collapse of the Confederacy had passed with enough semblance of order to hold out hope for a reunited people if everybody worked toward that end, he packed up his family and went with them to Europe to remain the better part of five years. He enjoyed the company of Dickens—whom he had helped to welcome in America—the company of Darwin, George Eliot and G. H. Lewes, John Stuart Mill, the Burne-Joneses, Matthew Arnold, Leslie Stephen, Ruskin, William Morris, Carlyle. "Yesterday," he wrote to G. W. Curtis concerning the pleasure of such friendships, "it was Leslie Stephen, the day before Frederic Harrison, the day before Carlyle, another day Morley, another Ruskin, another Burne-Jones, another Morris."

He seemed not to be at ease without the friendship of important men. Some of his American associates became pleasantly caustic about the matter. Did he not display his British friendships a little more than was required by the mere enjoyment of them? Possibly. Yet no one could deny that he valued them for what they were. He could speak admiringly; he could also speak honestly. In G. H. Lewes he found something which "reminds you of vulgarity." Ruskin he once summarized as "a kind of angel gone astray; meant for the thirteenth century, he got delayed on the way, and when he finally arrived was a white-winged anachronism." Of his numerous walks with Carlyle he wrote with affection, first of all, but also with penetration and shrewdness.

2

So the joy of spiritual self-indulgence had got the better of him, after all! So he was going to be an expatriate the rest of his days! To his American friends it so seemed. It might well have seemed so to his European friends. They liked him. At his best he was as nearly irresistible as any friend one might expect ever to meet. In the course of these years—darkened for him by the death of his wife—he had come to be a part of England, an expected figure on the landscape. All heated patriotism aside, there would have been logic in his remaining where he could enjoy friendships not to be had in his own country. Yet once again the inclination to get into things became dominant. He had seen much of the beautiful in the world; he appreciated the sustenance it may afford the human spirit; and he felt that his own country too little understood it as an element in civilization. Here was an idea to promote. But whether the best way to promote it was by living quietly as an example or by active dissemination, he had been much in doubt. Eventually he decided in favor of active dissemination. In this decision he was led by the gods into a destiny of great usefulness and great unhappiness. For he was to reënter America just when the country was beginning to exhibit the carelessness, the mental degeneracy, the uglification, that marked the last two or three decades of the century.

Photograph by Purdy

CHARLES ELIOT NORTON

He declared war... wherever he found it... ing it was climatically... His venerable first... where he was awarded... professorship in the... of mind by its rigours... university had recently... pressions of the unusual... presence a crude... They would meet... as long as let 2 and... Whenever he heard... he cried aloud in... the university not... tectural place. He... gestion of style. He... he could no longer... ugly building that... hour.

His face was captivating... pressions of respect... only be called serene...

He declared war. He would assail the ugly wherever he found it. And for his sharp eyes, finding it was almost the easiest thing in the world. His venerable alma mater, Harvard University, where he was prevailed upon to accept the first professorship in the fine arts, destroyed his peace of mind by its ugliness. The buildings that the university had recently erected were perfect expressions of the national apathy. He thought their presence a crime against the highest human nature. They would exert a degenerate influence on youth as long as brick and mortar would hold together. Whenever he heard that a new hall was to be built, he cried aloud in fearful anticipation. He begged the university not to be hasty in accepting architectural plans. He watched daily to catch a suggestion of what the lines would be. And when he could no longer keep from seeing that another ugly building had been added, he grew sick at heart.

His face was capable of two very distinct expressions: of warmth and something that could only be called sweetness, when he was in the heart of some intimate, steadying experience; of abject pessimism when he was annoyed and disappointed. About the university the undergraduates who did not come close to him, but only heard his protests against ugliness, saw much of the second expression. They thought him an over-sensitive malcontent. And they invented stories designed to express his groanings. He disliked Appleton Chapel with a hotness that approached enthusiasm. So they told how Charles Eliot Norton died and went to heaven, and how St. Peter begged him to come right in. But when he stepped inside he was overwhelmed by the brilliance. "Oh! Oh! Oh!" he exclaimed, shading his eyes with his hand. "So overdone! So garish! So Renaissance!" When St. Peter told him that if he did not like heaven there was only one other place for him, he said he believed he should prefer to go there. And he went. But soon he was back. "Well! Well!" said St. Peter. "You here again?" "Yes," Norton assured him, "and I think I shall stay. You are over-ornate here, but down there I found I was going to have to put in eternity looking at Appleton Chapel."

His greatest anguish came when it was decided to erect a building for his own large department. This building, he naturally expected, would be as beautiful and as perfectly adapted as it could be made. Was it not to be a house of the fine arts? But his distinguished cousin, who was then president of the university, and certain members of the Corporation, had their own notions of what the building should be, and they erected it over his protests. Despite all that has been said about it, the exterior was not so bad. But it was difficult to use. "Had it been intended as an example of what such a building should not be," he told the Board of Overseers—and the public, "it could hardly be better fitted for the purpose." He declared he would never lecture in it—though he did. He did not wish to be seen in front of it. And he bewailed its mere presence with such eloquence that some undergraduate was moved to paint on the smooth limestone surface of it, "Norton's Pride."

He did not live to see the birth of the new architectural conscience that has struggled to expression at Harvard—a conscience in no small measure the result of his crusading. So far as he could see at the end of more than a quarter of a century of warfare, "there is, perhaps, not a single University building of the last fifty years, from the Museum of Comparative Zoölogy to the Memorial Hall, and from that to the Harvard Union, which, either by its beauty or by the peculiar fitness of its adaptation to its object, is likely to be held in admiration one or two generations hence."

In another way, too, he wanted the university to help reclaim the best of the human spirit. How the spirit of friendliness might be extended if college men—the cultivated men of the country—would only play together! He became the first chairman of the first Harvard committee on intercollegiate athletic sports. But he had overlooked one slight detail. Some of the young men in Harvard, Yale, and Princeton—not to mention other institutions—were not cultivated. Instead of gentlemen applauding friendly contests, there were mobs of duffers shouting along the side-lines, "Stick his head in the mud!" "Cave in some ribs while he's down!" "Send for the undertaker!" His life did not reach over into the expansive days of the twentieth century when the severance of athletic relations between two universities endangers business partnerships in New York and Chicago. He did, however, live through a period when he suffered popular derision for scrutinizing an intercollegiate football schedule too closely or inquiring too closely into the academic standing—if any—of men who participated in games.

But his fight for beauty and for comeliness of spirit in Harvard University was only one expression of his great desire to educate the majority. All about him he saw an uglification that he wanted to arrest. He believed that the public might be led to see what was going on before their eyes. Streams of clear water were being converted into factory sewers. The sky was becoming obscured in unnecessary dirt and smoke. The seashore was being cluttered up with every sort of cheapness. The mountain-sides were being denuded of their forests by men intent upon immediate profits. Especially did he fear for the future of Niagara Falls. Early he foresaw a time when the Falls would no longer be in the heart of a country landscape, but in a city. The waters of the Falls would be diverted to all sorts of selfish ends. Would not his foresighted friends help to save the sublime spectacle? Would not politicians help to make the region into some kind of national park? "Why, yes," his friends said, "the Falls ought to be saved. But they will be, won't they?" The politicians said, "Why, man, there's enough water going over Niagara Falls to make power for anybody who would ever want it, without reducing the roar enough to tell the difference." He later saw the region becoming urban as he had predicted. He saw the Falls steadily diminishing in natural splendor. The fight was lost, he admitted; but he must fight on, simply to save his own soul.

He saw the process of uglification going on in the political world, too. Until the decade of 1920 arrived and established a new record in political degeneracy, the years in which his old age fell were the most discreditable perhaps in his country's history. As editor of the *North American Review,* as one of the founders of the *Nation,* he had developed a sensitive political conscience. So what could he do but become active in political affairs when he saw the country in the hands of bribers, party bosses, political hangers-on? When he saw that half of the degeneracy resulted from incompetent political appointees, he joined in the crusade for civil service reform. And while this reform was slowly making way, he concerned himself with candidates and elections—from the most important national contest to the most modest in his own ward in his own municipality. It was up-hill fighting. Appearance was against him. He looked too much like a gentleman. The professional politicians whose notions of democracy were very inclusive, referred to him as the "kidglove statesman." He sometimes lost his temper and replied with hot subtlety which they did not understand. But they never baited him away from the essential business he was about.

His greatest political battles came when he sought to enlist the national government in promoting good will. In all the disappointments that he had suffered, he had not despaired of having his country assume the lead in generous conduct. He had almost despaired when President Cleveland issued his pronunciamento on the case of England versus Venezuela. How could such a chauvinistic display be harmonized with the dignity of a great, peace-loving government? Probably he was misled by Godkin, editor of the *Nation*, into a more critical attitude than the circumstances required. Still, look at the incident as he might, he could not see how his country had been exactly a model in international friendliness.

Despair came when he foresaw a war with Spain over Cuba. He believed that the idea of war had been trumped up by the Republican politicians as a means of getting some glory for the none too glorious national administration. The prospect filled him with rage and shame. People in Cambridge who knew little of his essential spirit, asked, "And now what is Old Norton kicking about?" He was ready to tell them. He thought such a war would be no more justifiable than the war against Mexico had been. It was bad in itself and it would be used as an opening to an imperialistic national policy fraught with the constant danger of inducing hatreds against us among other peoples.

Nor did he remain silent when the war came. A patriotic citizen was not obliged to yield up his conscience when his government entered upon a war that he believed unnecessary. He had thought the Civil War inevitable; he had given all that it was possible for him to give toward winning that struggle in behalf of the enslaved. But in the present instance what good was war going to bring that might not be had by friendly counsel and negotiation? He spoke openly. And when the occasion came, he discussed before the students of Harvard the fundamental duty of a patriot in war time. He doubted whether the time was at hand when college students should desert their preparation for peaceful leadership and enlist in an army that would certainly be large enough without them.

Newspapers made him out a traitor and a corrupter of youth. Clergymen eager to appear "vital" assailed him in the pulpit. Fellow citizens filled his mail with abusive and threatening missives. Politicians, weary enough already of what they called an old man's idealism, seized upon the incident with religious ardor. So this is the man who has been trying to reveal our deficiencies! This is what you might expect the country to come to if you gave professors of art a chance! Among his distinguished assailants was his college classmate, Senator Hoar, who declared that Norton was a dangerous influence, and that it was time patriots should rise up and make the truth about him known. At least one other politician declared that he deserved to be lynched.

3

He did not seem to be getting very far. But he had been learning something. He had been learning the same lesson which William James at this very time declared that he had learned: "The bigger the unit you deal with, the hollower, the more brutal, the more mendacious is the life displayed. So I am against all big organizations as such, national ones first and foremost; against all big successes and big results; and in favor of the eternal forces of truth which always work in the individual and immediately unsuccessful way, under-dogs always, till history comes, after they are long dead, and puts them on top." Norton had to accept James's conclusion. So far as making opinion over in any wholesale fashion was concerned, the big world was unmanageably out of hand.

All the while he had worked patiently, loyally with individuals. It had seemed such a slow, futile way toward the majority's salvation. Yet long before he had learned his lesson permanently, he had had intervals of assurance that this influence on individuals was the only thing which counted. So he devoted himself to teaching.

His classes were large. They were large for a variety of reasons. Certain men came to him already interested in the arts. Certain others wanted to be. Certain others for social reasons wished to know the difference between an Ionic and a Doric capital. Still others wandered helplessly in because "it sounded easy." He was not at all averse to having the loafers along with the rest. In fact he one day said, "I should like to see an increase in the number of these idle persons." He hoped they might come face to face with some ideals.

The men in his great noisy classes escaped without enforced labor. It took three hundred men—or four hundred or five hundred—several minutes to get seated. A wag once said that the lecture hour consisted of two parts: getting in and getting out. And when they were seated, what was he going to do about it? Always an explosion was imminent. One day he was unable to bring to class his own copy of a book that he had asked the men to buy and read and bring. So at the beginning of the hour, when the men were in their seats, he asked if some one would be good enough to lend him a book. There was an embarrassing silence; it seemed that there were no books in the room. But at last a shy, boyish student in the front row stepped modestly forward, and handed his book up to the professor. There was great applause. Norton placed the book on his desk and opened it. "And now," he added, his face bright and keen, "if somebody will be good enough to lend me a paper-knife, we shall be ready!" This time the applause was uproarious.

Some of them escaped, too, with nothing more than a hazy impression that the professor was enthusiastic about his subject. One such undergraduate—it is authentic history—began the course by labeling his notebook, "Fine Arts 3" with a flourishing scroll. At the end of three meetings, his complete notes consisted of the following:

"(1) Greece.
(2) Bully for Greece.
(3) There are no flies on Greece."

But few of them escaped without a strange refinement in their conception of life; few of them failed to discover in themselves an enthusiasm for the beautiful that they had never dreamed they possessed. He cast his sharp, clear gaze over the room and talked with magnetic sublimity about a world that their unseeing eyes had never looked upon. He read Dante with such affectionate reverence that undisciplined youths who customarily spent lecture periods carving initials on classroom furniture slipped away at the end of the hour and bought all of Dante's works. He spoke with such eloquence upon the high function of the imagination in life that men were ashamed to admit how dull and unimaginative their own lives had been.

Nor did he encounter the resistance of the great majority when he received students at Shady Hill. Always some of his most enthusiastic followers were filtering through to the quiet of his study. And until near the close of his life, all the students who could not go home from the university for the Christmas vacation were invited to Shady Hill for Christmas Eve. He received them with a graciousness that they will contend has never been equaled. After they were all there and he had learned something about what each one was interested in, he read the Gospel story of the birth of Jesus. He discussed with them all sorts of philosophic and social matters—not always hopefully—and drew them into the conversation. Then they were all guided toward the dining room—he whispered to the young men to see that the ladies (always a few "nice Cambridge ladies") were served—where they found such a supper as few of them had ever eaten. For his good taste was not limited to books and pictures. One underclassman from a distant part of the country, eager to express his appreciation of the unexpected New England hospitality, and ignorant of Norton's caustic remarks about the raw parts of the United States, said when taking leave, "This has been just Western!"

The succor he was constantly giving to individuals would in itself make a sufficient contribution for any man's four score years. If a young, disheartened teacher went to him to make confession of his failure, Norton's glowing face was so full of assurance, his calm seemed to be established on something so permanent, that the young man was certain to come away without even mentioning his discouragement, and with a great new resolve in his heart. If a lonely scholar arrived in Cambridge from Georgia or Kansas, Norton was sure to hear his story, to help him gain access to the libraries of

Boston, to purchase for him some precious volume or other not available in another way. "Take this with you," he would command with irresistible kindness, and he would press a beautiful volume into the youth's hands. Or when he heard of brave spirits in some village who were trying to develop an interest in good pictures, he would pack up some of his most prized ones and send them off to be kept until all who might wish to see them had had opportunity.

In Ashfield, where he spent his summers, he saw organized industry slowly taking away from the community its independence and energy. Inasmuch as industry, he could see, was destined to stay, he interested himself in counter activities to develop initiative. He helped to organize prizes for any kind of ingenuity in children—he published an illuminating leaflet on the subject—from "plain washing and ironing" to collecting pressed flowers, observing plants or wild animals, making drawings or models, doing work with a jackknife or other tool.

In Cambridge, too, he one day made the discovery of some new interesting individuals. Near Shady Hill certain Sisters in the Catholic Church established a hospital for incurables. Early he had believed that there was something sinister in the Catholic Church. Once he wrote half seriously to a friend that he believed he could roast a Franciscan or stab a Cardinal in the dark! But as he grew into middle life, he embraced free-thinking as his religious creed. And as he became more and more an untrammeled free-thinker, he became more generous toward the Catholic church. Possibly his devotion to the fine arts had entered into the case. There was a disintegrating ugliness in Protestant churches. The Catholic church sought to maintain a certain unifying beauty. He felt this difference. A young Catholic woman said he was the only non-Catholic she had ever known who seemed to understand the Catholic religion. In any event, these Sisters were helping to make life tolerable for the unfortunate; and that was a part of his creed as a free-thinker. So he mastered every detail of the enterprise, and became their counselor. He also went regularly on Sunday afternoon and read to the incurables so that the long wearisome period was converted into one of beauty and fugitive peace. The drama of a divided Christian church never developed a more ironic sub-plot of tolerance, good feeling, affection, than in the devotion of this man to his Catholic hospital, and the devotion of its founders to this non-Catholic, free-thinking benefactor. "If you had done nothing else in your long and useful life," wrote the Secretary of the Hospital Aid Society, "there would be sufficient cause at this time for the angel of life to 'write you as one who loves his fellow-man.'"

Nor did he need to trouble himself about the resistance of the majority either, when he labored in his own study. In this seclusion he found the world at its best. One of his disciples who occasionally caught glimpses of him at his desk was so impressed by the dignity, the beauty, and the essential importance of the scene that he said, "I would have given anything I possessed just to be that little dog of his in there, that had the liberty of the study with him." He spent years making his translation of the *Divina Commedia.* He spent other years making corrections which the less discriminating would have regarded as inconsequential. He also translated Dante's *Vita Nuova*. He edited the correspondence between Carlyle and Emerson; the early letters of Carlyle; the correspondence between Goethe and Carlyle; the Reminiscences of Carlyle; the Heart of Oak Books; the letters of James Russell Lowell; the poems of John Donne, and of Anne Bradstreet; the letters he himself had received from Ruskin. He wrote on *The Poet Gray as a Naturalist*; on the lives of his friends, James Russell Lowell, George William Curtis, and Francis James Child; on the Cathedral at Chartres; on Rudyard Kipling—whom he early thought important; and on a few dozen other matters. Saturday nights, early mornings, odd hours of all sorts snatched from crowded days, he turned to literary use.

4

Thus he grew into the Charles Eliot Norton of "the turn of the century"—the stooped man with the side whiskers and the sharp, glancing eyes; the "Old Norton" of whom everyone spoke and of whom most younger men spoke affectionately. These younger men wanted to know, now that he had been through it all, what philosophy he had formulated. He was not unwilling to tell them. He had found two things that sustained him. The first of these was courage. He had hoped America would see the need of spiritual refining. He had dreamed about the country continually. Yet the great majority had laughed at his dreams and made sharp jokes about the dreamer. For him it had been no joking matter. Like the immortal Knight of Folly, he had "too great a soul to make jokes. He was laughed at for his seriousness." Naturally he had to have courage—courage to face ridicule. But this was not all. An ugliness of temper was developing in the world—and in his own country along with the rest—that he was sure would sooner or later culminate in the greatest orgy of hatred that mankind had ever known. He did not live to see it come, but he saw with terrifying certainty that its coming could not be put off.

It was not easy to live trivially when one saw a great evil day bearing down upon one's fellows. One must have courage. And there was yet another reason. The tenets of the professed religious faiths had ceased to have meaning for him. In truth, he had come to doubt even the least personal sort of immortality. And when everything is reduced to a few feverish seasons upon an indifferent earth, is not man then great according to the courage he commands? One must have courage.

In addition to courage there was the love of a few understanding friends. He was always ready to discuss the support that friendship afforded. He counseled the young to make friendships among the elderly lest they become enmeshed in their own unwisdom. He counseled the middle-aged to make friendships among the young, lest they grow old and their old friends die and leave them solitary. Courage, that other requisite, was easy if there were a few bright spirits to guarantee one against pessimism.

In a mellowed regality which comes only with having enjoyed and having suffered much, he lived into an old age that he confessed did not hurt as much as he had thought it might. He served his university—circumspectly. He read scores of manuscripts for anxious young authors and anxious old ones. He lent his name to causes he deemed good. He heard the raving of politicians and smiled to think that they were no more potent than he. He chatted tranquilly, the youthful glow flitting across his face, with disciples who hurried to Shady Hill as soon as they arrived in Cambridge. He hired boys to gather bushels of acorns for the gray squirrels of Cambridge, hard pressed by urban civilization. And he read to his beloved incurables in the Holy Ghost Hospital. From his piazza he saw Cambridge steadily closing in around his woodland. But for his own time, all would be secure. He could still bend over his growing tulips, or watch the hermit thrushes in the fastnesses of his wild roses, or study as much as he liked the habits of the night-herons that chose to rest for a time in the tall pines below his dooryard.

VI

Cosmic Prospector

COSMIC PROSPECTOR

I

RAPHAEL PUMPELLY was a poet. He was none the less poetic because the accidents of life made him into a geologist. Geologic research gave him opportunity to sit on the mountain tops, and on the mountain tops, he was quite ready to confess, he got more education, more impetus to go on, than in any institution that man had devised. "I understood then," he wrote after he had watched a sunset from a mountain in Corsica and had sat entranced until the moon had come up and had mounted far into the heavens, "why Moses and Buddha sought inspiration on the mountain heights, why Jehovah forbade worship in high places, and why the American Indian must, on coming to manhood, live for days and nights on the mountain in communion with the great spirit; for only in the vast silences of nature in her grandest moods, can the soul become attuned to the harmony of the Cosmos, and think great thoughts."

To men who filled their little minds with trivial practicalities, he was a kind of magnificent alien. He was tall of stature. Throughout his adult life he wore an incomparable beard that reached well down toward his waist—a "golden" beard until it later became the gray beard of a patriarch. Though his face expressed a dignified kindliness, his eyes seemed always to be looking far. He strode about with easy self-forgetfulness, as though he were well at home in the universe. No one could escape feeling that here was an extraordinary man. No one could escape feeling that this man lived some sweeping career of extraordinary quality.

There are three records by which he ought to be remembered. To begin with, he himself left a voluminous account of what he regarded as the most dramatic part of his life. Reminiscences can rarely be relied upon as final commentary on what is significant. One need only to look over the list of forgotten volumes of poetry and drama and fiction that remembered authors in their lifetime regarded as their masterpieces, in order to see how widely a man may miss the mark in judging himself. But a man's record of himself gives at least the authoritative detail of his adventure. And when one culls from Pumpelly's *Reminiscences* the barest facts of his journeyings, they constitute a narrative that no novelist who cares for an obvious appearance of reality would ever adopt in his fictitional creations.

In Corsica, whither he had gone at the age of nineteen just for the fun of it all, he lived for weeks among the shepherds and bandits of the mountains. Late one night—or early in the morning—while he crept about in search of his mules in the blackness of a thunderstorm, a cleaving flash of lightning revealed him within a step of the edge of a cliff, with the wild Mediterranean hundreds of feet below. He heard the stories of the Pozzo di Borgo family—stories of treasons and loyalties and killings and the sacredness of hospitality that make Mérimée's *Mateo Falcone* seem but a simple tale—and of other families in the region. By good fortune he one day met the young head of the Pozzo di Borgo family, ancient enemies of the Bonapartes, and this man took him to see the room where Letitia Bonaparte, after enduring much hardship in the mountains because her family opposed annexation to France and had to flee, gave birth to Napoleon I. In Corsica, too, at a later time, he bought a pet mouflon—since it was in order for European students to have pets—and took him to the continent, where he engaged in a wild campaign of butting over dignified hotel guests, leaping to the tops of tables, and shattering plate glass mirrors in which he chanced to see himself. He was an expensive luxury; but he was unique.

Pumpelly was uncertain about a profession. One day in Vienna he saw a conference of scientists announced. He decided to attend. At the door he addressed an elderly gentleman and asked if it would be necessary to register. The elderly gentleman was kind; he insisted that the young American sit with him; and the young American showed him some notes he had made on the geology of Corsica. This gentleman was Noeggerath, the geologist; incidentally, Noeggerath the father of a family of twenty-five children, the gallant old Noeggerath of seventy who kissed all pretty chambermaids. Noeggerath accepted Pumpelly as a young colleague in science. He advised him to go to the Royal Mining Academy at Freiburg, and in general gave him such a happy push that he was forever to be a geologist—plus. But if destiny kept him glad that he had encountered happy incidents, it also kept him glad that he had missed others. He decided to go with a French scientific expedition to the Sahara Desert and wrote to ask permission. His letter evidently was too late. But he had no regrets. The expedition never returned.

As a young mining engineer in Arizona at the beginning of the Civil War, he lived where every moment was heavy with possibilities. You might look across the landscape and see a man making his way along a trail, look away for ten seconds, and then look back and see nothing more of the man than a crumpled heap in the dust. You might go to your camp some evening and discover that the atmosphere of quiet about the place had been induced by a band of Apaches who had left two or three corpses on the floor. If you could get your cook or your guide or your chance fellow traveler drunk enough to feel unrestrained, he might tell of twenty murders he had committed; of others contemplated; of his plans to murder you. An object yonder in the fading light toward which a house cat or a nervous horse looked inquiringly might be only a cactus; but it might be a cactus plus a man, or a lone man without the cactus, or one of a band of a dozen murderous Mexicans, or one of a hundred somewhat more murderous Apaches.

One of Pumpelly's associates, Grosvenor, walked out just before night to see what had become of a wagon of ore that did not arrive in the afternoon. He was slow in returning. Pumpelly and the third member of the group went to meet him. The cat that accompanied them became nervous and expectant, and they looked in time to see a figure vanishing in the growing darkness. They saw the wagon a little farther on by the side of the road. But they were alarmed by the silence. They were hesitant, and became aware that a figure—a naked body—was lying at their feet. It was Grosvenor. The Indians who had killed the men on the wagon had lain in ambush for anyone who might come to investigate. The lone scout seen vanishing in the darkness had been left to report if anyone else came out. They hurried away in the dusk and reached their hacienda just as the Apaches were coming into view.

The possibilities were growing too heavy. It was difficult to keep one's thought on mining. Pumpelly decided to risk his life in an effort to reach California. In the long journey there was not much opportunity for relaxation. Killers were everywhere. He was so anxious when he slept that he kept his hand always on the grip of a pistol. One night he discovered that he had been sleeping with his finger on the trigger of a pistol that was cocked. And if there were no capital dangers in the form of fellow human beings, there were petty annoyances—in the danger of finding no water on the desert, for instance; in five-foot rattlesnakes. One night, in order to enjoy the air, he and his fellow traveler Poston folded their blankets, stretched them out side by side, and lay naked upon them. After a time one of them moved slightly, and there was a husky buzzing between them. They leaped to their feet, seized a brand from the fire over which they had cooked their coffee, and in its light saw a rattlesnake disappearing in a hole under Pumpelly's pillow.

From such a life one required minor adventures to ease one down. They came. On the way from San Francisco to Japan—a commission from the imperial government called him there to make explorations for minerals—the heavily laden clipper ship on which he traveled struck a calm. Another ship, larger but lightly laden, was carried by the swell nearer and nearer and nearer until destruction seemed inevitable. But just when the great hulk was towering over them, a slight breeze came along and carried it safely by. In Hakodate when the Russian Consul gave a masked ball, Pumpelly, dressed in the armor of a Japanese warrior, mounted a rearing, plunging horse, and rode up the high flight of granite steps to the Consulate— an approach that no horse had ever before made.

From a Drawing by Margarita Pumpelly Smyth

RAPHAEL PUMPELLY

In Shanghai, where the cholera raged, he spent fascinating hours in bric-a-brac shops. Aboard a boat on the Yangtze-Kiang he helped to fight off enraged Chinese soldiers who were determined to take possession. The sight of human bodies, floating in rigid humility down Chinese rivers, led him to wonder how many Chinamen were buried in the sands of the Yellow sea. After a night spent in an inn where he had arrived late and had gone to bed in a narrow compartment in the dark, he discovered that he had slept between two wall-like piles of coffins.

Stricken with smallpox, he lay for a fortnight in wild delirium: "I was on a horse and chased by mounted Indians along the crest of a jagged mountain range. In mad flight, springing from peak to peak across valleys and gorges, I looked back on a thousand Apaches racing in single file. Yelling, hair streaming behind, flourishing lances, that file of painted devils, sailing through the air, were pressing me close, returning my pistol shots with showers of arrows. At last a chasm too broad to span! Midway we fell, my horse and I; down we went whirling like a wheel. I looked up; the Apaches, too, were whirling downward. I looked down; from far below there arose the roar of a mighty torrent dashing over rocks. Instant death was there—unless I could screw an eye open and see the bedpost."

The abrupt disappearance of his first Chinaman nurse and then of his second; the discovery of a revolver under his mattress, and then the detection of bullets imbedded in the walls of his room were sufficient evidence that the delirium was not without solid elements of reality.

In a trip across the Gobi desert in the dead of winter, the problem that confronted him was simple: it was to avoid freezing to death. He traveled seventeen hours a day; he rode and he slept in a specially designed sleeping cart which, despite abundant robes, was so cold that a bottle of hot coffee wrapped up beside him would freeze in the course of the night if it were not hugged close to his body. In Siberia, where the thermometer sometimes registered seventy degrees (Fahrenheit) below zero, he decided to set out alone by sleigh for Moscow. At one of the stations the day after he started, he was asked if he would take a fellow traveler. He assented. But he was a little astonished to learn that his fellow traveler was to be a woman. He found consolation in the fact that she was young—scarcely eighteen—and that she was beautiful. Rolled into two great bundles that could recline in the sleigh, and assured of fresh relays of horses and drivers, they traveled day and night, with only respite enough for the changing of the horses and drivers and for meals. She spoke only Russian; he spoke no Russian at all. But from the great interesting bundle he learned a few words each day.

The long stretch of succeeding nights and days merged in a pleasant idyllic detachment—the detachment of which only youth is capable. "It was sometimes not easy," he said, "to make out whether my companion was asleep or awake, especially in the morning, nor was it an easy task to make preparations on my own part for finding this out. In the first place, there was the usual necessity of thawing out one's eyelashes. It was only after this, and pulling down the great collar of the outer robe, and rolling over on the left side, that I caught sight of my companion, or rather a mountain of shapeless furs towering beside and above me, and issuing from the top a small spiral column of vapor like that which betrays the wintering place of a bear. How was one to know whether sleep or wakefulness existed under these motionless robes? The mother of invention taught me a ready expedient. Lighting a cigarette, I puffed vigorously till I felt sure that every fold and crack was penetrated by the aroma. It was a sure test, for my companion, like most Russian ladies, was passionately fond of smoking, and never could resist the temptation. If she was awake, a gentle movement was soon perceptible, ending after a while in the appearance of a small hand with a cigarette stretched out to be lighted. In this way the time passed smoothly enough, which is more than I can say of the road."

At Petrograd he learned that he had traveled with a Polish lady of noble family who had been in Siberia to comfort her brother, an officer in the

Polish army of rebellion who had been condemned to life sentence in the Siberian mines.

Nor did his "striking coincidences" end with his youth. In the long level stretch between forty and fifty when little is supposed to happen in a man's life, he had to be content with nothing more exceptional than seeing five mules roll eight hundred feet down a steep mountainside with no damage except to the packs they carried. But as an old man he saw things lively again. On a southern river he took the daughters of his closest friends for a camping trip on a raft of lumber that moved slowly down toward the sea. One day the young ladies, weary of safety, proposed that they take to the water and swim along behind the raft. Pumpelly agreed on condition that they attach themselves to a long rope which he was to hold so that they might not fall behind. But an alligator made for them; and Pumpelly could not pull the rope fast enough. Only a bullet from the rifle in the hands of a negro who had rushed to the rear of the raft prevented the alligator from having a morsel or two for his unwonted effort.

But after all, these "striking coincidences" were only details. He recognized their abundance in his career. He not only wrote them down and published them—in *Across America and Asia* and in his *Reminiscences;* he talked about them to any whom he chose to admit to his circle. Yet they were only a by-product. That which gave distinction to his place among men, that which rounded his career to valid significance, was a long series of contributions to men's practical comfort and to liberalizing knowledge. These are recorded in volumes of scientific research which a reading public never sees. Such volumes never excite the multitude—unless to contempt for highbrows—though the multitude is forever profiting from them. Go into the street—it is a bewildering experiment—and begin to ask men who Raphael Pumpelly was. You will quickly discover how lonely the explorer is in the crowd. Some will tell you that Raphael Pumpelly was an ancient artist; some that he was a popular novelist. But most will have no knowledge of him at all. He was of the elect company whose individual lives are quickly—or slowly—absorbed in the impersonal life of the times that follow them.

Yet the record which he left in the Smithsonian Institution, in journals devoted to science, in ponderous tomes published by the Carnegie Institution, in letters to his official superiors, is alive with imagination. From some mountain top he was ever viewing the present, the past, the future, with new and quickened largeness. Before he was thirty he had awakened interest—scientific and industrial interest—in China, Mongolia, and Japan. He was appointed to the first chair of mining at Harvard University, and from that official post—though it paid little and limited his movements little—he had new opportunities to make geology significant in the affairs of his country. In the late sixties and early seventies of the nineteenth century, men with money to invest were looking for advice—were ready to rely upon the judgment of anyone except themselves. Pumpelly foresaw the age of steel. He advised them to search for iron rather than gold. Some of them followed his advice. Some of them, with his scientific aid, made millions of dollars. He might have made some millions himself; but he never regretted the more modest course of a man of science which he pursued instead.

His comprehensive view of the earth resulted in his being called into all sorts of gigantic, significant enterprises. In the northern peninsula of Michigan—one of the places where the man in the street does know who he was—he outlined the Menominee and Gogebic iron regions and had the satisfaction of seeing some of the great mines of the world developed there—mines that in his lifetime brought millions of tons of ore into the new world of steel. He became State Geologist for Missouri and made valuable preliminary surveys there. He directed the census of mineral industries of the United States in 1879-80, and, certain that iron was the basic metal in civilization, gave special attention to iron. Later he was made a counselor to the National Board of Health. The country had become alarmed at the number of deaths that seemed to result from underground pollution of drinking water. Pumpelly, because of his geological training, was asked to direct an investigation. He and an assistant worked for two years on sources of pollution, and on the filtration capacity of various soils and other materials. But Congress abolished the Board!

One other vast American inquiry in which he lost himself happily for two or three years was the Northern Transcontinental Survey. The letters on the subject have been preserved. They reveal his great enthusiasm for the project; they show how conscientious an explorer he was in estimating the value of what he and his associates found. Henry Villard, full of dreams of a network of railroads in the great Northwest, engaged him to report on what there might be in the northern Rockies that would attract men and commerce, and therefore provide something for the railroads to haul. He and his associates covered an extensive area, looking for steam coal and anything else that might be useful to a man interested in railroads. Some strange two or three ideas became associated in his mind one day, and he was seized with a desire to carry the exploration into the Alaskan coast. In one of his letters he pointed out how the venture might be useful and how a very modest sum of money would carry on the work. But Villard's whole dream came to a crashing financial end—though he later recovered in most heroic fashion—and the survey, for want of imagination on the part of other railroad officials, was promptly abandoned.

But men as well as the ways of cosmic forces interested him. Perhaps if one were to get down close, one might discover that what men did was much more a part of cosmic life than the men suspected. He began to look with a new element in his looking.

When he had made his early trip across Asia, many geologic facts established themselves in his mind with distinctness. For the remainder of his long life he was constantly turning them over and using them as beginnings. One theory that he early evolved from this experience was that the central portion of Asia had at one time been a great inland sea. Eventually, as his hypothesis took form it was stupendous. He believed that in the known glacial periods of the earth's history, the great ice-cap to the northwestward had poured abundant water down into the bowl of central Asia and kept the bowl well filled. With the passing of the long glacial periods, this abundant source was reduced to nothing. Not only that; the region is surrounded by a mountain wall that permits little rain to come from the oceans. So the waters of the great sea, in the course of thousands of years slowly evaporated. At present all the water has disappeared except in such bodies as the Aral Sea and the numerous small lakes that, like water holes after a flood, are inevitably vanishing. With the sea gone, and with currents of hot air rising from the sun-baked surface of the region, the little moisture that could get inside the mountain wall would not condense in the form of rain. The aridity of the region, therefore, became greater and greater until it reached its present state of relative balance.

Now as the sea receded in this long, long process, civilizations might have developed, Pumpelly thought, on the fertile oases made by the streams where they emerged from their canyons on to the plains. In fact, men of nomadic habits might have pastured their flocks for long years in the basin itself before the aridity made the region too desert-like to support such life. As the aridity became greater and greater, there would naturally be searches for new pasturage—movements toward the better-watered regions. Possibly these movements outward from the center of the dry basin were the beginnings of migrations destructive to the people who had developed a stabler life in the regions that were better watered. Possibly these movements gave the initial shock that, passed on, became the Asiatic invasions of Europe. Possibly enforced migrations originating here had brought to Europe Aryan peoples and therefore Aryan language and culture.

It was an enchanting hypothesis. If only he could go to Turkestan. If only he could study the geology of the region more thoroughly and excavate for traces of forgotten civilizations, he might convert the hypothesis into established fact. He organized an expedition—when he was past sixty-five. The Carnegie Institution financed it. For two years he and his corps of distinguished associates devoted themselves to reconnaissance and to excavation. The geology of the region supported his theory. The excavations might. He directed the sinking of shafts in the kurgans at the oasis-city of Anau. Pottery and implements and other stray memoirs of man's activities enabled him to trace civilizations back to very remote centuries—yet when "man at Anau already lived in cities, cultivated wheat and barley, began the domestication and breeding of the useful animals which are our inheritance and possessed the fundamental arts, including a certain amount of metallurgical knowledge." The evidence seemed to be adequate to prove that here was the home of objects and practices that only later were to be found in other parts of the Western world. The slow desiccation of a vast region had pretty certainly resulted in movements which had exerted an influence—even a constructive influence—on other parts of the world. It was enough to make an elderly man happy.

But if part of the findings offered a new explanation of the past, another part offered both an explanation of the past and a possible forecast of the future. In early middle life he had come to believe with Richthofen that loess, the fine, almost microscopic dust that makes up the fertile soil of parts of Russia, northern China, and southern Mongolia, is distributed by winds rather than by water —except as water sometimes carries it from mountains to dry plains where the winds can get at it. The great loess-producing region of interior Asia, then, will provide somebody with loess as long—so far as man in his tiny view can see—as the present Asia exists. Only some sweeping climatic change which would deprive the region of its aridity would stop the process. The winds whirling across the dry surface of the desert—a surface that the sharp heat of the sun slowly prepares for the winds— catch up clouds of material, sift it according to weight, and carry the lightest particles farthest. Back and forth the clouds are carried, but in the course of a year they are carried farther and farther northeast until they come to a region where there is firm vegetation, which acts as a net on the surface of the earth, and the loess is held just where it is needed to give the vegetation sustenance. The endless process has covered not only plains but the surface of mountains—mountains five thousand feet above sea level. In northern China, Pumpelly reminds us in one of his reports, it has covered much of the country to a depth of hundreds of feet. He reminds us also that it has produced crops year after year for several thousand years, "practically without fertilizing additions."

His concluding inference is sobering. In the economic struggle that must become more intense as the earth becomes more thickly populated, the nation that will fare best eventually will be the one that has the most permanent soil. Most soils wear out quickly if used without respite. Loess does not. The United States, except for Missouri, Iowa, and the Dakotas, is not much blessed with loess. China, with a fourth of the world's present population or more, a population that has developed great vigor and potential capacity in its struggle with its very overabundance, has much of this self-fertilizing soil with no prospect of a diminution. Who knows but what China may one day be in a position to speak with imperial authority?

So, if he could live the life of an adventurer, he could also live the life of a dreamer of majestic dreams. He could enter into necessary acquaintance with fields of science related to his own—archæology, for instance—with such a sure mastery that certain people wondered if he were not some kind of facile charlatan. He could shut himself up for two or three years and digest material for his reports. And he could write of his explorations with a sensitive regard for the intelligent general reader that has been exceeded only by Darwin or Huxley—if at all.

3

Yet he left another record without which his adventures would seem distortionate, his explorations motiveless—the subtle yet clear impress of his inner self. It is a less tangible kind of record than the other two, but his intimates would say that it is more significant than either—or both.

For those who were much with him had opportunity to discover with some completeness what the casual wayfarer who chanced to meet him felt but vaguely: here was a spiritual aristocrat. In one respect the literal-minded who pronounced judgment upon him were right: he was an alien. He would have been an alien anywhere. But especially was he an alien in the bustle of the New World. The innate aristocracy of his spirit was evident in the most casual moment of his daily round. One day he rode a prancing thoroughbred through Beacon Street in Boston. His own manner as he rode, erect and contemplative, his great beard parted a little by the breeze, made clear that he, too, was a thoroughbred. A young man watched with bulging, half-amused eyes, wholly intent. Then he muttered to himself: "Golly, what a swell!" Such a figure might belong in some remote, expansive region where patriarchal philosophers thrive, or in the broad avenues before some towering palace, but not in a narrow street, not in a crowd.

His dignified, immaculate appearance was in

character; for all his thinking was aristocratic in flavor. He had no "line" of small talk. He could not listen to gossip or chit-chat and be concerned. He cared not at all for discussions of politics; the trivial-mindedness of politicians as a class was too evident. He cared little for athletic sports—except horseback riding. He cared not at all for indoor social games. What he liked was to sit with Clarence King, or James D. Hague, or Henry Adams, or Henry Holt, and discuss the future of the Rockies, the future of the Pacific, the future of the Orient; or to engage in long, exciting discussions of anthropology or archæology; or to speculate upon human survival of death.

He reverenced the great mystics of history. Without laying claims of any sort, he was a mystic himself. He felt that we are so intimately a part of the inclusive and not unfriendly spirit of the universe that this spirit is constantly making itself felt within us, constantly "intervening" to our benefit, when we do not offer too much active resistance through our little hatched-up notions of what the universe ought to do in order to treat us beneficently. He believed in a stupendous immortality.

To his untrammeled mind, religion was an exciting field for exploration. He was too much of a pioneer to be a conformer. He did not go inside churches. He thought people who busied themselves with churches were chiefly small-minded persons rattling loosely around at something which to him was utterly barren or even destructive of an important spiritual life. Yet he cherished the conversation of religious men—an occasional Protestant clergyman, an occasional Catholic priest, an occasional religious philosopher from the Orient. Oriental philosophies, he believed, if abruptly adopted in the Western World, might overtopple our sanity, perhaps. Still he found in them something eventually reassuring. His life was not wholly taken up with mouflons and Apaches and Polish countesses and iron ore and coal fields and vanishing inland seas. Some day, after he had had time to bring all his reflections into orderliness, he meant to write his views on religion.

In every matter, he preferred the long view. The permanent value of a civilization, he contended, could be estimated by the capacity it developed in men to refrain from hasty conclusions, hasty rewards. When he walked with his grandchildren—and he had a vast assemblage of them in all—and they asked him, as if they were addressing a god, why it rained, he never explained directly. He would begin by asking them questions in turn—questions that called for long periods of observation—and they were soon so excited with the project of eventual discovery that they were on the direct way to becoming educated beings. When somebody came to him with a scheme that guaranteed immediate returns, he was not interested. Things did not work out that way. What he wanted to concern himself with was the project that fifty or a hundred years ahead would be approaching fruition. "This is a sound idea," he would explain. "It will work out. We shall never see anything come of it; and our children will not. But our grandchildren may; and our great-grandchildren are sure to." The method has disadvantages; he never, for instance, got quite ready to record his religious views—except fragmentarily in conversation. Still the long view was the only one worth the attention of a civilized man.

Yet more than in his thinking the aristocracy revealed itself in his emotional life. He was constituted with such a sensitiveness that any kind of cunning or petty gratification brought him pain rather than pleasure. If men wanted to run over him, very well; he did not intend to besmirch himself by running over them. There was in human life something that ought to be respected. In men who labored long days with their hands, he found an essential gentility. In women of humblest class, he found an essential beauty. From his youth he was sought—even pursued—by assiduous women; he had full opportunity to see that not all women belong in the age of chivalry. Yet he treated them all with chivalrous respect—even those who did not deserve it. His feeling for fellow mortals, for all living things, grew into a sublime pity. A man who had faced cunning and death more times than a veteran of wars, would not so much as take the life of bird or rabbit.

His magnanimity brought him the devotion of

miners, mule drivers, farm hands, secretaries, nurses, chauffeurs, neighbors, and colleagues. It also brought him the esteem in which the true aristocrat is held by the pseudo-aristocrats. They asked jauntily, "Where does the old man get that line, anyhow? Does he think anybody is going to believe that there isn't something under all of his fine uppishness?" When he told about the journey across Siberia, and left the inference that it never became more than a youthful idyll, they laughed with a fine leer and asked themselves, "Don't we know his kind?" But he only smoked undisturbed as he looked away across the lake and said to himself, "I guess they don't."

He belonged to the old school; he loved his wife—with abandon. When she was well enough, she went with him on his expeditions—to Lake Superior, to Turkestan. Always he looked after her with the solicitude of a young lover in a fairy tale—acting as body guard, as nurse, as a kind of super-servant. He taught all children and grandchildren to open and close doors silently, to walk without touching their heels to the floor, so that they would not disturb the sleeping goddess. When she grew old—though she was years younger than he—her possible going was something he could contemplate only in pathetic bewilderment. He must forever be near to care for her, to shield her, as he had always done. On the day of her death, he had absent-mindedly tied a bright oriental scarf over his bare head to protect himself against the draft from the open window as he sat by her bedside. When she had gone, he was disconsolate—but not because of his own loss. He paced the house like some heroic wraith, his white face and beard all the whiter against the bright scarf, and mourned that she should have to be on some long journey alone where he could not be present to look out for her.

He gathered his children about him and went away to the desert and the mountains of the Southwest. Although he never recovered from the loss of what he called the "most important factor in my environment," he was still the poetic explorer. The sight of the region where he had done his first adventuring in America fifty years before gave his mind a new keenness. He was full of ideas about iron, about soils, about the control of the lower Mississippi, about anthropology and archæology and philosophy. He talked more intimately. He became a little more accessible. His children had always looked upon him as a creature quite too godlike for any rough-and-tumble familiarity. They still maintained a worshipful attitude toward him; but now he seemed a little less remote. One evening when he and one of his daughters were alone, he said to her: "You know my life; I have told you much about it. Now tell me about yours—everything." And they sat the night through while she, a woman of early middle years, recounted, and he, a man of four score and more, listened and questioned and commented. He found the experience amazingly interesting, and he confessed that he learned much.

The mystical in him became more pronounced. He felt attracted by any mind that seemed to draw generously upon sources below—or above—consciousness. Geology, full of implications about all life; archæology, full of others; philosophy, full of still others, afforded days and nights of stimulating conversation. But he was never most at home when he was with people. He never found any mind so quickening as silence, nor any acquaintance so fascinating as the unknown. The spirit of his youth and of his old age—for they were one—was summarized when he rode solitary across the Pamir, the "Roof of the World," and contemplated the desolation of Lake Karakul; or when he climbed to the more modest rocky ridge of Mount Monadnock above his summer retreat and sat bareheaded in the early autumn sun, his cane dropped lightly by his side, the thumb of his closed hand pressed against his chin reflectively, and his blue eyes, inquiring but undisturbed, looking away toward the Green Mountains to the westward.

VII

A Sublimated Puritan

A SUBLIMATED PURITAN

I

THE most heroic display of courage in New England was not at Concord Bridge or Bunker Hill, but in Mount Holyoke Female Seminary. Principal Mary Lyon had just made her announcement to the young ladies assembled in chapel that Christmas was to be celebrated as a fast. After she had awed—or bullied—the hesitant into acceptance, she asked—that is, dared—any dissenter to rise. And Emily Dickinson stood up.

Merely to be the solitary dissenter required courage enough. Unsympathetic eyes on every side, supported by stout authority, have driven many a college girl to surrender convictions that she had believed were laws of nature—and possibly were. Unsympathetic eyes on every side, without the official support, have caused many another to turn away from college broken-hearted. Emily Dickinson did not choose to surrender. Nor did she decide to go home—except for a rebellious celebration of Christmas. Instead, in a little world where it was proper to think as the majority thought, and where the majority had much of its thinking done by somebody else, she dared to express the sense of fitness cherished by the minority.

But her courage was far greater than that necessitated by any mere rebellion against the established order. She sought to carry on a rebellion that was selective. Some of the established order she would keep, some of it she would discard. She was not warring, for instance, against religion; she was warring against the absurdities of religious practice that had attached themselves to the church. Her revolt was not against the whole of Puritanism; it was only against that part of Puritanism which she considered senseless and ugly and debasing. From what she found all about her she would select elements to meet her individual needs.

Three quarters of a century later it is still possible to see the hazard of her undertaking. America, after all, is in very much the same state of mind now that it was in then. It is easier than not—just as it was then—to participate in the opinion of the majority. A few bright catchwords that sum up favorable or unfavorable attitudes of mind are all the stock in trade required. Everything is labeled in fool-proof pigeon-holes: Radicals, Evolutionists, Wets, Fundamentalists, Prohibitionists, Highbrows, Puritans. In order to make anyone out an enemy of society it is only necessary to apply the right epithet with enough of a leer. Today the Puritans happen to be the "outs"; the majority is fixed in its belief that nothing Puritan was ever important. In Emily Dickinson's day the Puritans happened to be the "ins"; the majority was just as fixed in its belief that everything Puritan had always been important. The pigeon-holes have been reranked. But the partitions have not been rearranged or broken down. When one professes to feel a little at home in a number of them— or in none at all—the world is aghast. Those who have incidentally pigeon-holed themselves in the process of pigeon-holing everybody else become warlike, or glacial, or contemptuous. How can busy people be expected to form an opinion of anybody who is not labeled? The first necessary step is to label her; the next, to keep her labeled.

And if the mere process was difficult, the material on which she was to exercise choice was more difficult still. In the Puritan spirit there was a confusing mixture of good and bad elements. The Puritan was hard—just how hard one may see by encountering certain of the New Englanders who have survived the Irish invasion. But his hardness made for simplicity; and simplicity is not without its advantages. He was forever shearing the complex down to austere fundamentals. There must be no over-ornateness in his houses—still among the most beautiful in America; or in his churches—quite the most beautiful still; or in his worship; or in his speech; or in his recreation. With a terrifying God in heaven where was there any room on earth for sentimentality?

The Puritan carried himself mightily. If he did not display purple and scarlet in the grand man-

EMILY DICKINSON

per, he at least wore the best broadcloth that money could buy. His linen and silver were the envy of every one—he meant them to be—and they still are. And he required plenty of servants to do his bidding. But if he was haughty, he was also self-respectful. He admired men's weaknesses —and women's—but he meant to be weak just as little as possible, and to say as little about it. Most of the time he could see himself well up to the scale toward his oft-quoted God. If it would not do for men—just fewer than average—as rôle in the performance of his high fate, wot?

The Parvan was remote. Above timely interest has gone to an untimely grave because he refused to be disturbed. But he was also given to a very profitable "outworldly" way of thinking about life. He was inclined to view things in the large. He might miss some of the petty irregularities of the nearer landscape, but he could failed to make a fair estimate of the horizon. He built his house only when he was able to have the kind of house a man of dignity might to occupy. With that house ner, he at least wore the best broadcloth that money could buy. His linen and silver were the envy of everyone—he meant them to be—and they still are. And he required plenty of servants to do his firm will. But if he was haughty, he was also self-respectful. He admitted men's weaknesses —and women's—but he meant to be weak just as little as possible, and to say as little about it. Most of the time he could see himself well up in the scale toward his all-powerful God. It would not do for man—just lower than the angels—to flag in the performance of his high function.

The Puritan was remote. Many a timely interest has gone to an untimely grave because he refused to be disturbed. But he was also given to a very profitable "unworldly way of thinking about life." He was inclined to view things in the large. He might miss some of the petty irregularities of the nearer landscape, but he rarely failed to make a fair estimate of the horizon. He built his house only when he was able to have the kind of house a man of dignity ought to occupy. With that house in view, it did not so much matter whether the intervening years were perfect or not.

He was sorely deficient, too, in his understanding of pleasure. He reasoned—so it seems—that because tinsel is sometimes of a parcel with pleasure, everything pleasurable must therefore be tinsel. But if he was unsensitive to the need of pure recreation, he was aware of the buoyance that comes from getting the essential business of the world done in good order. If he did not know the ecstasy of sweeping along just for the sheer joy of it, he did know the somewhat solemn satisfaction of having earned his bread without resorting to graft, of having given bread to those in need, and of having maintained a proportion in life that saved him from remorse.

Now when the mere exercise of choice was something to make one tremble, and when the choice was to be made from a vast array of such elements as these, could Emily Dickinson make headway? Could she save the simplicity without too much of the hardness? Could she maintain an unfailing respect for herself yet remain honestly humble? Might she enjoy a little of earth while waiting for all of heaven? Could she scrutinize an entire accepted order, take what her conscientious self dictated, and forget the rest?

2

No one would say that she surrounded herself with a world that was profuse. She knew little enough about what was going on in Boston or New York or London or Paris. But it was a world full of intimate reality. Right in her own house there was a diversified family to understand. Her father was a stern, well-dressed gentleman—a lawyer and a member of Congress—who got up from his chair and walked silently out of the house when Emily said or did anything that he disapproved. In her own words, his heart was "pure and terrible." She missed her brother Austin when he was away because there was no one else who appreciated jokes and poetry so well. Her father, she explained to Austin, seemed to believe that about everything was "real life." Her mother was somewhat overshadowed by a strong-willed husband. But she had neuralgia, and in other submissive ways provided Emily with something precious to think about. Emily baked the family bread—because her father was disinclined to eat that baked by anyone else. Emily made choice cakes and puddings. Emily made ice cream. Emily followed the activities of their two dozen hens with a housewife's anxiety. Once she called attention to the fact that the entire twenty-four would "do nothing so vulgar as lay an egg."

Her family, too, included sister Lavinia. She was fascinating, coquettish. When relatives arrived unexpectedly at meal time, Lavinia could command a resourcefulness that became legendary. She could hold off troups of admiring Amherst College students with a fine skill that made them tenfold more restless in their contemplation of her. No one can look at her photograph without a complete understanding of the symphony of sighs she created in a college town. She was, according to Emily—or perhaps Emily's mother—capable of demoralizing the life of a dog. And the dog would enjoy the experience. She heartened the whole household. "I, you must know," she once remarked to a neighbor, "am the family inflater. One by one the members of my household go down, and I must inflate them."

And above all, as it turned out, there was Susan Gilbert Dickinson, Austin's wife. Somewhere out of the heaven that sometimes sends good to men—and incidentally to women—Susan one day appeared. For the rest of Emily's lifetime, Susan was to be the great understanding spirit that called for more and more poetry. When she arrived in Amherst as a bride she created a disturbance. She was accused of metropolitan ways and of worshiping strange gods. But the town, and not Sue, had to surrender. She was irresistible. The elder Dickinson found that she made better coffee than he could get at home. And Emily, long after she had completely withdrawn herself from the broader thoroughfares of the world, kept the path bright to Sister Sue's house.

When the family of individualists was not claiming her personal attention, she had letters to write.

Letters gave her opportunity to assume all sorts of fantastic rôles. She signed herself "Poor Plover," "Vinnie's Sister," "Your very sincere and *wicked* friend," "Your Scholar," "Marchioness," "Your Gnome," "Your 'Rascal,'" "Barabbas," "Modoc," "Emilie." For her correspondence was carried on with men and women who called for ingenious powers of adaptation: Mr. and Mrs. J. G. Holland, Mr. Samuel Bowles, Judge Otis P. Lord, Maria Whitney, Louisa and Fannie Norcross, Helen Hunt. And she outdid herself in flirtatiousness in her letters to Thomas Wentworth Higginson. Upstairs in the singing quiet of her own room, she could be as brave as anyone. To write to somebody far, far off was almost as simple as expressing oneself out into space—or into the great capaciousness of Sister Sue's heart. No inharmonious resistance deterred her. She devised valentines; she discussed religion—sometimes gravely, sometimes cheerfully, sometimes whimsically; she offered congratulations to the victorious, and sent pathetically beautiful notes to those who had suffered; and she characterized with unforgettable detail the most intimate and the most remote members of her family. She characterized herself. She might, she thought, be the belle of Amherst—so she confided to Mrs. Strong—by the time she was seventeen. She wondered—on another occasion—if she were not Eve. Why not? she asked. Since there is no record of Eve's death, might it not be true? By the time she was thirty-one and had been stared at when not dressed in her more usual calicoes, she was revealing her own awareness that she had become a character in the eyes of the people about her. "Won't you please tell 'the public' that at present I wear a brown dress with a cape if possible browner, and carry a parasol of the same!" A year later (1862) she included in a letter to Colonel Higginson the sketch of herself by which she was later to become known: "I am small, like the wren; and my hair is bold, like the chestnut burr; and my eyes, like the sherry in the glass that the guest leaves."

If her family and her letters were not claiming her devotion, she could observe Amherst village, and such other parts of the world as might come into view. When she still attended church, there was opportunity to regard the world in miniature while the minister sought in prolonged effort to make the earth so full of terrors that anybody would be glad to escape to heaven. She went to Northampton to hear Jenny Lind, and enjoyed the bewilderment of her austere father who listened beside her—to the Jenny Lind who carried away from Northampton for this recital four thousand dollars plus expenses. She enjoyed the excitement of a village fire; she found days of ecstasy in one glimpse of a circus in the street. She watched the miracle of the aurora borealis, the miracle of every new night and new day, the miracle of the marching seasons. She watched the industrial age come to her dooryard by means of railroads. She saw the whole tragedy of the Civil War in the funeral of one Amherst boy killed in battle.

She made only a few excursions out into the noisy world, and these were not inviting enough to be kept up. There were glorious things to see, but everybody seemed to be hurrying and nobody thinking. And from one of these trips she returned with a new terrifying problem. She had met a man who brought the great storm to her heart, as she did to his. It was better to keep close to one's doorstep.

But like every sensitive soul, she could learn much from little. She invited a singer in a church choir to come and sing for her. The young woman came, with her brother and sister. Emily stayed upstairs to listen. But later, in the library, she told the young woman that she had not met the brother, but that she distinguished his whistle as he trudged along the street. Family conversation, snatches of life that floated upstairs to her when visitors were below, the sight of people as they went about their daily chores, the commentary of the Springfield *Republican*—from such sources her expectant mind caught up as much of the narrative of contemporary life as she required.

3

But such a little world! Such a pity that one with so capacious and faring a soul should not have lived a life more expansive!

Yet, after all, did she miss anything of the importance? Did she miss anything by electing to remain in seclusion? She did not think so. She enjoyed the monastic peace. A thoughtful neighbor, young and responsive to the open air, once asked Lavinia why she did not induce Emily to go out a little. "But why should I," Lavinia answered. "She is quite happy and contented as she is. I would only disturb her." And the cosmopolitan point of view was something she was not fearful about. Anyhow, did one acquire it simply by running toward the point of greatest clamor? Yonder, across the hills, a nation was busy with "progress." An industrial age was remaking everything in a hurry. A new political age had developed unawares; the men who had grown up with the Constitution were gone and their successors were now trying to decide whether the Constitution stood for cohesion or disintegration. Men and women were hastening away by thousands to pursue some end of the rainbow in the Mississippi valley or on the Pacific slope. College undergraduates were everywhere debating the question, "Resolved, that the man of action is more important than the man of thought," and the affirmative was the popular side of the question. She preferred the quiet room upstairs, thank you, and the path under the elms to Sister Sue's house, and her unmolested opportunity to listen to the winds and the rain and the birds, and to see the apple blossoms come and the cherries ripen and the maple leaves turn to flame on the mountainside. Why did people want things so dreadfully cluttered up? Why did they enjoy taking so many steps to get nowhere? For after they had spent a life on the rumbling treadmill, who among them could stand forth and point to any real progress he had made?

Or had she missed anything by renouncing the orthodox trappings of Puritanism? Always she had possessed the Puritan's capacity for self-discipline; if she had willed she could have brought her own spirit, rebellious and whimsical as it was, into subjection. But now in the twentieth century eclipse of the Puritan spirit it is easier than not to see how fatal such subjection would have been. She was not by nature an orthodox person; not even the seclusion of an orthodox convent would have satisfied her. Ready-made organizations were not designed to make her feel at home. Nothing could be conceived more foreign to rightness than an Emily Dickinson who dressed with pretentious conformity, carried a hymn-book to church every Sunday, voiced approval of a God who took infinite delight in punishing his children, and as a repressed little old maid offered commentary on the trivialities of the oncoming generation. It is sacrilege even to think of it. One grand final heartbreak would have been heaven for her compared with such a slow death of torture.

Or did she miss anything important when she refused to rush into a renunciation of the whole of Puritanism? Suppose at Philadelphia when she met face to face the one man—the young husband—who swept her into an unpeaceful sea, she had adopted the immediately easy formula that one must live one's life regardless of whom it kills. Suppose she had proclaimed with a grand flourish of feline selfishness that she knew no law other than that of her own nature, and had fled with the young husband—as much overwhelmed as she—when he pursued her to Amherst. As a mere matter of ability later to salvage anything acceptable from what the earth had to offer, would she have been ahead? It was all tragic enough, in any event. But would it not require a gross mind to say that for such a sensitive soul as hers there would have been a grand total of more satisfaction in having had her own way at the bitter expense of somebody else? Where would she have found anything more to be cherished than the integrity of spirit that sprang from the uncomplicated memory of the experience, the even-tempered contemplation of what a more friendly fate might have brought to her, and the firm putting aside of the ordinary for the sake of the ideal?

4

But above every other word of testimony that might be adduced, stand her own poems. She is a perfect instance of the writer whose poems are more intimate than letters. In her poems she dealt with matters so close to her that she could mention them only in the impersonal—and then guard the manuscript throughout a lifetime. And these poems reveal no pathetic creature to be pitied by the champions of some expanded life. Things were flitting away, certainly; but did one catch more of them by rushing about trying to encompass them all at once? Things were not passing in such torrential chaos that one had to let go in a great spontaneous yowl or go down unexpressed. When one began to push the non-essentials out of the way, life became warm and tense and endless. Then there was "a lonesome fluency abroad, like suspended music."

She made—we cannot escape the discovery in her poems—more than a scientist's acquaintance with nature. She lived in an exciting world of iris and orioles and daffodils and cocoons and butterflies and robins and snakes and daisies and clouds and sunsets and snow and hemlocks and dews and wells and mountains and lightning and revolving planets. She became more and more a philosopher and made shrewd observations on greatness and littleness; on the demoralizing effect of too much joy; on the joylessness of those who have never wanted; on the comeliness of victory to those who have never won; on the air of improbability surrounding the story that one has actually lived; on the singular way men have of showing more respect for a corpse than for a living person; on pain; on peace; on the attitude of the undiscerning toward the discerning; on the completeness of death; on immortality. She was at once an entranced cousin of Fabre and a sweet-tempered distant relative of Schopenhauer.

In her poetry, too, one discovers her great intimacy with her own spiritual life. So much did she live with hope and skepticism and love and pain and death and birth and friendship and labor and the outlook for immortality that she was more at home with these than anywhere else. They were so much a matter of daily experience that when she wrote about them she seemed to be expressing the experience of anyone who would read. Two score years after her death anchorites read her verse and find in it an obvious justification for their religious solitude; fearful persons find assurance not only of the reality of their own fears, but of the reality of their own timid hopes; the trivial-minded profess to discover that her lightness is akin to their own; men and women who gropingly toil without escaping perplexity see in her heroism a way to grim but abiding consolation; and young poets who have not lost their enthusiasm or begun to develop a malignant encrustation of spirit hear in her every page a sympathetic admonition to go their own authentic ways.

Naturally out of this intimate spiritual life that Emily Dickinson lived, there developed in time an immediacy of approach to everything. No indirectness blurred her impressions. "If I read a book," she told Colonel Higginson, "and it makes my whole body so cold no fire can ever warm me, I know that is poetry. If I feel physically as if the top of my head were taken off, I know that is poetry. These are the only ways I know it. Is there any other way?" Her approach to the most baffling, the most sublime matter, was just as direct:

> "Say, Jesus Christ of Nazareth,
> Hast thou no arm for me?"

Death and God and pain and hope were tremendous considerations, but they were nothing to get panicky about. "She would have been quite capable," declared her niece, "of offering God her sweetest flower or her frailest fern, sure of His acceptance." If reality rubbed elbows with one all the time, why should one be afraid of it?

She achieved freedom. Sometimes the Hound of Heaven pursued her; but not for long. For she would turn on him and say such unanswerable things to him that he looked shamefacedly away and wondered why he had been pursuing her at all. She could take liberties unafraid. She could be fantastic, caustic, coquettish, piteous, loving, grave, humble, worshipful, without leaving anyone convinced that she had gone too far. She discovered that her own modest, reconstructed soul was just as much to be relied upon as souls that were less reconstructed, and less modest.

So natural was her freedom—freedom in contemplation, freedom in manner—that those who found unfreedom comfortable did not discover that she was free at all; she had not kicked loose with enough of a flourish. Thomas Bailey Aldrich could find only intermittent flashes of imagination in her, and thought her admirers had mistaken a simple New England bluebird for a nightingale. But as it became more and more fashionable to seek freedom—even though somewhat rapaciously—it became easier to see how she had been, and is, and for long will continue to be a source of faith for those who would find the fullest intensity and highest honesty of their own spirits.

5

It was a world worth making for oneself—and others. Things in that world were transubstantiated into pure poetry, pure significance. We have now come to believe that it was a romantic world. Something that refuses to become sentimentality, yet something that even the disillusioned think upon as aromatic of old lavender, clings to the story of the slight little woman who secluded herself for a quarter of a century or more, and then slipped quietly from the earth, leaving the old mahogany bureau full of poems that were some day to gladden thousands of understanding hearts. But for the soul that had to save itself from both Puritanism and Puritanism's antipathy, and that had to resist being warped into something resentful and ugly by a practical society, it was more than old lavender; it was myrrh and it was hyssop.

VIII

Lincoln the Radical

LINCOLN THE RADICAL

I

He probably would find the twentieth century as difficult as he found the nineteenth. New York City would vote against him, as it did in 1860. Highly respectable citizens in every other part of the country who boast their loyalty to the great tradition of Abraham Lincoln would cast their ballots for somebody else. They would rally to the support of Stephen A. Douglas. For Douglas was an evenly balanced person, a man of judgment, a practical man. He believed in accepting things as he found them. He wanted to know why people couldn't be happy in the nation as their fathers had made it. But Lincoln was lop-sided, engrossed in things as they ought to be, full of visionary and dangerous ideas. Lincoln was a radical.

He passed through the inevitable sequence of the radical with as little deviation as if it had been made especially to fit his single career. He began—the first phase of his sequence—as the poet of the world. He sang the joys and tragedies of his own life, and touched the life of others into a quickened, unfamiliar tempo. It is libel to say—as is commonly said in the turmoil of city streets—that his early surroundings were drab and restrictive. He lived at the heart of one of the most dramatic migrations known to the modern world. The Ohio river and its tributaries were alive with all sorts of rude craft. Expectant families felt the limitations of poverty and social inferiority vanishing as they contemplated wooded hills and rolling green plains that stretched away westward to infinity. Caravans were ever winding through the gaps in the hills, ever wading through ague-haunted lowlands, ever braving the devastation of tornadoes and the icy suffocation of blizzards—all on the way toward some poetically remote objective.

It was a time for going a little farther than anybody else had gone. There was invitation in whatever required men to extend themselves to the limit.

From photograph lent by Herbert W. Fay, Springfield, Ill.

ABRAHAM LINCOLN

Torrential streams were made to be crossed—by anybody who was strong enough—or followed to their extremities; hills were to be climbed; trees of unimagined circumference were to be felled; fields covered with stumps were to be cultivated; strangers appearing upon the landscape from nowhere in particular were to be tested in strength; settlements active with romantic, muscular people were to be investigated; great fresh silences with moist—or hot—breezes playing through them were to be meditated upon for significant flashes of meaning; cities of amazing grandeur in countries they would never see, were to be read about—by the fortunate ones who could read—and marveled at; enemies possessing the most dramatic shrewdness were to be anticipated and outmatched by unfailing alertness. Life was expansive. No thin plating of sophistication restrained the spirit. No apartment house made men too much at ease to see the poetry of the road that leads from a log cabin.

In such a world everything called for a remaking. Everybody was in some manner engaged at the task. With an ax and a maul and wedges it was one's romantic privilege to contribute to the history of civilization. In Indiana it was a current saying at that time—and much later—that a man who could not take a rifle, an ax, a horse without harness, and a pair of plow-shovels into the woods and with such a beginning produce everything man's comfort required, was no man at all. Fields, houses, utensils, food—all had to be wrought from the abounding earth. Trails had to be converted into roads; streams had to be explored and made useful; cities had to be firmly planted; bridges had to be built—eventually; railroads had to be dreamed of and sought after. County governments had to be developed; courts of justice had to be established; means of a rude education had to be discovered—and as many other means as possible devised for saving to the greatest number of human beings the most fruitful freedom of spirit.

This transformation Lincoln saw taking place everywhere about him. And from the time he was old enough to engage in any self-directed movement he participated in it. As he grew to lank manhood he was especially fascinated by the prospect of making over the spiritual life of the people. As a candidate for the Illinois legislature he stood for education "as the most important subject which we as a people can be engaged in." He had, too, idealistic dreams about other changes that ought to be wrought. By the time he was twenty-seven, he had gone on record as favoring woman suffrage. By the time he was thirty-three he had gone on record concerning two other matters. "And when the victory shall be complete," he said near the close of a speech on Washington's Birthday, 1842, "when there shall be neither a slave nor a drunkard on the earth, how proud the title of that land which may truly claim to be the birthplace and the cradle of both those revolutions that shall have ended in that victory!"

Strange dreaming, was it not? But in the vast silent spaces of early Illinois, it was easy to disengage an idea from its entangling surroundings and look at it with steady eyes until its outlines became unconfused. The world he saw was illimitably blessed with the glory of imperfection. Might not one conceive of all sorts of changes to be made—changes for the better? And might not those changes be brought to pass at almost any time? If a man could put his hand into a barrel of rubbish that he had bought—because he wanted the empty barrel—and bring from the unpromising depths a copy of Blackstone's *Commentaries*—a book destined to change his life from that day forth—might not the whole human family be groping around within reach of all sorts of significant possibilities? Long before he ever came upon Walt Whitman's *Leaves of Grass,* he was dreaming of a new democracy that would touch sleeping mortals into life. In a world where so many things could be remade, why not remake the social order?

2

To him his views seemed reasonable beyond question. When he had had nothing else to do he had turned them over in his mind without end. But not everyone looked upon them with such approval. Some persons declared them dangerous and out of place. Not only that. He began to encounter active resistance on the part of organized forces. How anyone should wish to war on plain honesty of thinking he could not understand. Yet even here in this unmade country were institutions that did not want anybody to think too much or too clearly about them, and that did not want to think about themselves at all. He found himself regarded as unusual. He found himself standing more or less apart. So without wholly ceasing to be a poetic dreamer, he passed into the radical's second phase: he became a heretic.

His heresies extended to all three of the fields in which he was accustomed to dream—to politics, to social customs, and to religion. By nature he was one of the most religious of men. In a certain fundamental sense which the passively devout cannot so much as understand, he was a Christian; that is, he believed with Jesus of Nazareth that the way to find a satisfying life is to seek for it, as little fettered as possible by the categorical thinking of anybody else. He did not accept; he inquired.

And when he sat down in the expansive atmosphere of central Illinois and inquired for a God comprehensive enough to satisfy his needs, he did not find him in the religious denominations. The terrifying monster preached about in the pulpits had nothing in common with the great beneficent spirit of the universe before whom he sometimes threw himself in anguish. So in religion he came to be the bad boy of his neighborhood. Nobody could trick him into making a formal confession of his sinfulness. Nobody, not even the resourceful Peter Cartwright, could browbeat him into declaring for the literal, tinsel heaven delimited so scrupulously by delimited minds. A half century and more after his death, men still write about Lincoln the Free Thinker, Lincoln the Mystic, Lincoln Man of God. And he was all of these. That is why the church looked upon him as a suspicious character. That is why, according to his own count, only three of the twenty-three ministers in Springfield stood ready to vote for him for President of the United States.

His heresy in social life consisted of a contempt

for pretentiousness. It was not a new heresy. Thomas Jefferson, whom Lincoln once referred to as the man "who was, is, and perhaps will continue to be, the most distinguished politician in our history," had himself tried to think in terms of an unpretentious national life. But after all, Jefferson was an aristocrat—in part, at least, by defect of his times. By the middle of the century, however, the common man had begun to come into possession of some small part of his inheritance. There was a better opportunity to carry a theory of unpretentiousness into practice. If there was to be a certain essential equality among men, should not as many as possible of the artificial barriers between them be broken down? Ought not the official classes divest themselves of useless trappings? Would not the people find a new incentive to intelligent citizenship in the new unpretentious candor?

But even in his own provincial region, neither the official classes nor the people were ready to surrender the pleasant glamour. If the Honorable So-and-so, or General So-and-so, was preceded with enough awesome whisperings, he was certainly a great man. Douglas, a becomingly dressed bulldog of a little fellow with a resounding voice, rode in special trains, paid gallant compliments to ladies who needed them, and referred to all sorts of distinguished political and social connections "back East" in the most effectively casual manner. How could anyone doubt that he was a powerful thinker and a man of taste?

Lincoln offered his heretical protest. Pretense blinded men and women to reality. So he sat around as much as he liked with his coat off; he talked with the humblest who spoke to him with an intimacy of understanding that gave them a respectful sense of equality; he traveled without telling anybody that he regarded himself as a man of potential importance; he rode—when the demands of campaign required—in a caboose with trainmen; and he exercised his sharpest satire on those in high places who sought to be awesome. "By the way, Mr. Speaker," he observed with biting casualness one day in Congress, when he had been flaying General Cass as a make-believe military figure, "did you know I am a military hero? Yes, sir; in the days of the Black Hawk war I fought, bled, and came away." The times were yet against him. People to whom simplicity should have made appeal expected a distinguished person to have an exterior unlike their own. In the very business of fighting their battles for them, Lincoln had to engage in a long, silent struggle with them in order to prove that his manner was something they should be proud of instead of something they should disdain.

But these heresies might have been forgiven had he not avowed another infinitely more disquieting. At a time when it was not only fashionable but politically expedient to speak tactfully about human slavery—to pretend to think of it only as a matter of economics or geography or climate—he openly began to assail slavery as a moral wrong. He meant to say what he thought. He meant to reveal just what the country's record had been in matters of human liberty. And what had that record been? "As a nation," he wrote to Joshua F. Speed in Kentucky, "we began by declaring that 'all men are created equal.' We now practically read it, 'all men are created equal except negroes.' When the Know-Nothings get control it will read 'all men are created equal, except negroes and foreigners and Catholics.' When it comes to this, I shall prefer emigrating to some country where they make no pretense of loving liberty—to Russia, for instance, where despotism can be taken pure and without the base alloy of hypocrisy." The trouble was that slavery had become socially sacred. He meant to divest it of its robes of sacredness and reveal it as a mighty and hideous figure of death that was touching all of men's political thought with its own corruption.

In the process, he did not hesitate to snatch the purple from other idols, or to make wry faces at them. He assailed the President of the United States. The President, he contended, had been a party to an unjust war against Mexico. In his single term as congressman from Illinois he demanded in his Spot Resolutions that the President show the exact spot on which the war began.

Everyone was entitled to know whether the war at the outset was a Mexican invasion of Texas, or a United States invasion of Mexico. Was he not shockingly impudent? But he was destined to go further. A little afterward (January, 1848) he made a speech in Congress in which he assailed what he called "the sheerest deception" of the President's reasoning. Point by point he took up President Polk's argument and showed how the President was trying to befog the real issue; how he was "trusting to escape scrutiny by fixing the public gaze upon the exceeding brightness of military glory—that attractive rainbow that rises in showers of blood. . . . How like the half-insane mumbling of a fever dream is the whole war part of his late message!"

Nor did he, in those dozen years before the Civil War restrict his incidental assaults to Democratic presidents. He assailed the Supreme Court. He believed the Dred Scott decision was a legal monstrosity. It held that a slave was property; that a man had a right to take property wherever he chose; therefore, a slave owner had the right to take a slave into a "free" territory and keep him there—as a slave. Lincoln believed that this decision was narrow and prejudiced and corrupt. It was, he contended, political rather than legal. All the circumstances—including the Court's withholding of the decision until after the election of 1856, and the incoming President's exhortation of the people to show good spirit by accepting the decision when it came—pointed to an understanding, a conspiracy, on the part of the Court, the outgoing and incoming Presidents, and certain United States Senators. They were quietly working together to extend slavery to every part of the Union. His charges were declared to be more insolent than his speeches against President Polk and the Mexican war. It was not then fashionable to lock men up for questioning the infallibility of the courts, but he received enough condemnation on the part of his political enemies—headed by Senator Douglas—to keep his mind pleasantly occupied.

But he did not mollify his charges. He had been about courts more or less himself; and he had been a little in the world of politics. Judges sometimes made wrong decisions; they occasionally admitted the fact themselves. And judges were sometimes politicians—a fact which they did not so often admit. Sometimes the politician got the upper hand and made the decision. So why should the judges and Presidents and senators make him out such a pariah just because he had seen through the tricks in this particular instance? They thought they had covered up their tracks; they thought they had worked with undiscoverable secrecy. The frame of the new structure which they had in mind had been carefully cut at different times and in different places. But it had been done with full concerted understanding—"all the tenons and mortises exactly fitting"—so that some day the actual completion of the structure would be perfectly simple. He could not prove his charges, but he knew they were true, and he meant to say so.

And now that one began to think of the matter, other declarations that he had made in the same period assumed a disturbing character. More heretical than any specific charge against the existing administration was his pronouncement upon government in general. He had declared that "any people anywhere being inclined and having the power have the right to rise up and shake off the existing government, and form a new one that suits them better. This is a most valuable, a most sacred right—a right which we hope and believe is to liberate the world." He contended, furthermore, that a chief revolutionary may put down minorities, as we of the Colonies put down the Tories in the course of our revolt against England. Did he believe that this theory was universally applicable? And just what significance was there in his further observation that "it is a quality of revolutions not to go by old lines or old laws, but to break up both and make new ones." When he uttered these words they were only a part of his brief congressional career that the voters of Illinois were not inclined to prolong. But now he had become one of the two most important political figures in the state. His reputation was going to other parts of the country—especially the South. Might it not be well to keep in mind his recorded utterances?

There was nothing in his entire attitude that was very respectful to the constituted authorities. His enemies—including Douglas—openly declared that while he was in Congress he had opposed sending provisions to the United States army in the war against Mexico. They stretched the facts beyond truth. But he did make himself so annoying, and he did stir up so much dissension over the Mexican war that the people of Illinois were ready to consider somebody else for the next term of Congress. And this doctrine of revolutions—did it have any part in his open warfare on slavery? Did it have anything to do with that declaration which everybody said he had made but which was not a matter of public record—the declaration before the first state Republican Convention (1856) to the effect that "we will say to the Southern disunionists, we won't go out of the Union, and you *shan't*"? Was he not on record as disturbing pretty nearly everything?

But he became more heretical still. Just at the time when the South had become so jumpy and so threatening that wise politicians were saying that if the Union were to be saved it would be necessary not only to leave slavery unmolested but to say nothing about it, Lincoln came forward—in the state convention that named him as its candidate for United States senator—with the benumbing pronouncement not merely that the Union ought not to be saved on that basis, but that it could not. The country could not endure permanently half slave and half free. "A house divided against itself cannot stand. . . . I do not expect the Union to be dissolved; I do not expect the house to fall; but I do expect it will cease to be divided. It will become all one thing or all the other." Was ever utterance more untimely? Here when two or three political wizards had devised all sorts of intricate compromises and balances to keep everybody satisfied, Lincoln was stirring everybody up by saying that the efforts of the wizards were of no avail. Not even his friends—except Herndon—could approve this new position. They had always regarded him as an astute politician. Yet here he was proposing to throw the conservative vote away before the campaign started.

More amazing still, he proposed to wage his campaign by means of a series of debates with Douglas, who sought reëlection. Douglas stood sublimely "for the Constitution and the preservation of the Union." His statesmanlike position attracted attention throughout the country. As far east as New York City, Horace Greeley thought the people of Illinois ought to keep away from the "idealistic" Lincoln and swing their support to the sagacious, practical Douglas. But now Lincoln would provide his own destruction if he insisted on giving the Little Giant a chance at him. Douglas assented to one debate in each of the seven congressional districts of the state provided he should have the advantage of opening and closing the discussions four of the seven times. He would keep faith with the fathers and show the people exactly how much statesmanship there was in Lincoln's prejudiced sectional doctrines.

Perhaps no other man in America was capable of doing it better. Douglas was clear-headed; he was an able speaker; he was shrewd; and he possessed a quality that every politician prays for—

plausibility. According to some, Douglas would "make mince meat" of Old Abe before the debates were half over. Just how he meant to do it was indicated in a speech he had made at Bloomington some days before the exchange of letters that resulted in the debates. "Although the Republic," he declared, "has existed from 1789 to this day, divided into Free States and Slave States, yet we are told that in the future it cannot endure unless they shall become all free or all slave. For that reason, he says, as the gentleman in the crowd says, that they must be all free. He wishes to go to the Senate of the United States in order to carry out that line of public policy, which will compel all the states in the South to become free. How is he going to do it? Has Congress any power over the subject of slavery in Kentucky or Virginia, or any other state of the Union? How then, is Mr. Lincoln going to carry out that principle which he says is essential to the existence of the Union, to wit: that slavery must be abolished in all the states of the Union, or must be established in them all? You convince the South that they must either establish slavery in Illinois and in every other free state, or submit to its abolition in every Southern state, and you invite them to make a warfare upon the Northern states in order to establish slavery, for the sake of perpetuating it at home. Thus Mr. Lincoln invites by his proposition, a war of sections, a war between Illinois and Kentucky, a war between the free states and the slave states, a war between the North and the South, for the purpose of either exterminating slavery in every Southern state, or planting it in every Northern state."

As for himself, he had abiding faith in the wisdom of the fathers who had made the country half slave and half free. He believed that that was the only basis on which the nation could endure. Many parts of the country wished slavery, and this was a nation in which self-government was guaranteed to the people. When territories became states they could decide for themselves just what they preferred in the matter. It was all perfectly simple. Why, then, should Lincoln go about in an effort to incite the people? He himself would never do so. He cared not whether slavery was voted down or voted up. It was purely a matter for the people to decide. Could anything be more reasonable?

Tens of thousands wanted to be present at these gigantic tussles. They drove through the dust and mud of the prairies to the encounters nearest where they lived. They spent uncomfortable nights in their springless wagons or on the ground under them. They stood and listened through long hours in the August sun and the October chill.

At the outset the Little Giant proceeded to do what was expected of him. He rushed into Lincoln and put him on the defensive. He called upon the people to rally to the support of the constituted authorities and the country as the wise fathers had made it—half slave and half free. He warned them against the menace of sectionalism. He would not have one region array itself against another. And especially did he warn them against making the black man in every way the equal of the white. He himself held no brief for equality. "I do not regard the negro as my equal, and positively deny that he is my brother, or any kin to me whatever." And as for the Declaration of

Independence, when it is said that all men are created equal, he did not believe the signers of it had in mind "the negroes, the Chinese or Coolies, the Indians, the Japanese, or any other inferior race"!

They heard his maxim-like arguments with applause. He was living up to expectations. Still he did not demolish Old Abe. When Lincoln stood before them, his shoulders covered with the dust of travel, his voice pitched higher than seemed natural for such a rugged man, they found him interesting. He was not so obvious as Douglas; his point of view required close attention. But he seemed more reasonable than they had expected. He was not hoping for war. He was not certain that there would be one. But he was certain the country could not go on indefinitely in its present state of uncertainty and distrust and compromise. As for the revolutionary-minded fathers who had freed themselves from England and made a Constitution of their own, they had put slavery where they thought it was in the course of ultimate extinction. Had they not provided for the end of the African slave trade? Had they not prohibited slavery in the Northwest Territory? "Why stop its spread in one direction and cut off its source in another if they did not look to its being placed in the course of its ultimate extinction?" And had they not been careful to avoid any reference to slaves as such, so that when the days of slavery should ultimately pass, there would be no embarrassing traces of it to humiliate a people whose government supposedly had been founded in human freedom?

The trouble was that the question had been reopened—at the time of the Missouri Compromise and at numerous times since. The South had been zealous in keeping the question open. And the Dred Scott decision, by making it possible for a slave owner to take his slaves—his property— with him into a territory, was intended to keep it open until the institution had become established in every part of the country, North as well as South. It had made slavery legal in a territory, despite what the people of the territory might vote. It had reduced Douglas's pet theory of popular sovereignty exactly to the thinness of "the homeopathic soup that was made by boiling the shadow of a pigeon that had starved to death." So far as the territories were concerned, it simply meant "that if any one man choose to enslave another, no third man shall be allowed to object." And who knew, if we accepted this dishonest ruling of the Court as a sacred "Thus saith the Lord," that we might not wake up some morning and find that the Court had ruled that a slave owner could take his slave—his property—not merely into a territory but into a free state. And then if we accepted that decision as we had been counseled to accept all decisions of the Court—as a "Thus saith the Lord"—slavery will have become impregnable in every part of the country.

So the country had come, after all, exactly to the place where he said it had come; to the place where it had ·to decide whether it preferred to become all slave or whether it preferred to limit slavery with "ultimate extinction" in mind. In the crisis, he was not going to be neutral. He favored "ultimate extinction." He did not propose to molest slavery in the states where it was established. But if it were not allowed to spread, and all the new territories should be free territories, eventually the atmosphere in the United States would become an atmosphere of freedom and the institution would slowly pass out of existence without economic upheaval. But slavery was a moral wrong, no matter how many of one's good friends happened to be in the business, and he would enter into no proposed compromise that accepted it as a moral right. Compromise had already done its utmost, and that utmost had been unavailing.

Ought he to be sent to the Senate of the United States? The people of Illinois did not quite think so. Douglas was returned. But Lincoln had been heard. Especially had he been heard in the South. And the South understood Lincoln. "If such an enemy of slavery ever goes to the White House," the people of the South said, "we will go out of the Union." What did it matter if he had declared that he had no intention of molesting slavery where it existed; if he meant only to prevent its spread and to put it where it would be in the course of ultimate extinction? When a man is sentenced to death, does he find much comfort in being assured that it may not be strangling at all, but starvation? The South thanked him for his honesty in making clear exactly where he stood.

His defeat did not deter him. Nor did the menacing attitude of the South. Nor did the clamour of many Republicans who were fearful. He had liked that "house divided" speech from the first. "If I had to draw a pen across my record and erase my whole life from sight, and I had one poor gift or choice left as to what I should save from the wreck, I should choose that speech and leave it to the world unerased." And he was not going to be stampeded by his associates, the South, or anybody else.

He went to Columbus, Ohio, and in a speech in reply to an article by Senator Douglas in *Harper's Magazine,* reiterated the doctrine. Douglas had said that if the people in a territory did not want slavery, they could exclude it by local police regulation even if the Supreme Court had held it legal to take slaves there. Lincoln riddled the argument, which, he said, resolved itself into this absurdity: "that a thing may be lawfully driven away from where it has a lawful right to be." And so far as Douglas's caring not whether slavery was voted down or voted up, the doctrine was quite in keeping with Douglas's character. "He is so put up by nature that a lash upon his back would hurt him, but a lash upon anybody else's back does not hurt him." At Cincinnati he expressed the same doctrine—with variations defiantly addressed to the Kentuckians. At Leavenworth, Kansas, he went further and let it be known what might be expected if the slave states should try to secede when he chanced to have anything to do with the matter. "Your own statement of it is that if the Black Republicans elect a President, you 'won't stand it.' You will break up the Union. If we shall constitutionally elect a President, it will be our duty to see that you submit. Old John Brown has been executed for treason against a state. We cannot object, even though he agreed with us in thinking slavery wrong. That cannot excuse violence, bloodshed, and treason.

It could avail him nothing that he might think himself right. So, if we constitutionally elect a President, and therefore you undertake to destroy the Union, it will be our duty to deal with you as old John Brown was dealt with."

At Cooper Union, smarting under the clamorous accusation that he was a revolutionary, he placed great emphasis upon his ultra-conservatism: he agreed with men as old-fashioned as the revolutionary founders of the nation! That he was one with those rebellious spirits who favored putting slavery where it would be in the course of ultimate extinction, nobody could deny. But calling himself a conservative on that account was only a neat way of forcing his opponents to assume the burden of proof—if they would. Radical and conservative are not estimated according to the beliefs and practices of the preceding century; they are estimated according to the beliefs and practices of the time when the question is up. The people of the South who lived in his time did not think— could not think—according to beliefs held in 1776 or 1787. For them the "existing order" was the contemporary status—the one in which slavery was accepted and allowed to have very much its own way. That that was the temper of the times Lincoln himself had often declared. So when he proposed a restrictive policy, even if his proposal did chance to accord with a view held in the eighteenth century, he and not the South was the revolutionary.

Ought he to be made President? The South had no illusions on the subject. The best they could hope for, in so far as he might have authority, was "ultimate extinction." Slaveholders had just as much reason to expect him to be generous toward slavery as legalized saloonkeepers would have to expect generosity from a fair-minded but ardent temperance reformer. They did not need to reason it all out in cold blood; they could feel the unfriendly atmosphere descending from the northward.

The border regions begged for a candidate and a platform that would be conciliatory. "A little conservatism on the part of the North," John Speed of Louisville wrote to Henry S. Lane of Indiana in 1859, "would secure a large vote in several of the slave states." As a platform, he thought opposition to acquiring further slave territory, non-interference with slavery as it existed, opposition to the African slave trade, internal improvements by the federal government, and any pleasing generalities that might be "inserted as matters of taste," would be about right. Other platform makers farther north likewise proposed planks designed to reach across the Ohio river. And in the lists of presidential possibilities, Lincoln's name was not always to be found. Many who believed that Seward could not carry states with a border population as large as that of Indiana and Ohio, proposed that Lane himself be the candidate. He had won respect and admiration as the permanent chairman of the first national Republican convention. "My impression," wrote one of his correspondents in a letter explaining why Bates and Cameron and Reed and Fessenden and Pennington would not do—the last named for the brief reason that he was "an egotistical old granny"—"is that either Lincoln or yourself could by some exertion be nominated. I think you have a better record and as good a location." But Lane, a clear thinker and a man of sensitive conscience, became convinced that Lincoln ought to be named. With zeal he gave him that great necessary first support outside Illinois that convinced the country at large that Lincoln was more than a "favorite son" candidate.

Through such loyalties, through certain eastern enmities against Seward, and through "breaks" in the political game, Lincoln was nominated. Through such loyalties and through other "breaks" in the political game, he managed to receive approximately 1,850,000 votes out of approximately 4,650,000. But when the 2,800,000 votes against him were conveniently distributed, his votes were enough to elect him. He would not necessarily have been defeated had all the opposition centered in one candidate instead of three. Still, the victory was not very flattering. In the South, his opponents received something like fifty times as many votes as he did. In the North their combined votes were only three hundred thousand behind his own.

Douglas alone had received almost two-thirds as many votes in the North as he had. No one could call him a popular hero. Yet here he was, elected to a position where his theories concerning revolutions and minorities would be put to the test.

3

As he approached his new high office, he entered upon the third phase of the radical's inevitable sequence: he became a spiritual solitary. At the head of any organization the radical is always lonely enough. But in Lincoln's case there was a special element that counted for loneliness. He was to carry his point—if he carried it—by waging a war. Not only that. He was to wage a war for what, after all, was an unpopular cause. Roughly speaking, almost half of the voters in the North had disavowed his stand on the slavery question. Those who did adhere to him were of all shades of confidence and doubt. Now that he was to grapple with the problem, they felt utterly detached. "Poor Old Abe!" they sighed before he went to Washington to be inaugurated. "He has a tough job on his hands." As though it were not their job, too!

So what he had been in personal idea he now became in official fact: the lone head of a revolution—against human slavery—in the course of which he had to suppress a minority—the South. Those who were to come after him might devise all sorts of ingenious explanations to account for the Civil War, but he and the South had a perfect understanding on the matter. They were to decide whether slavery was to go or to stay.

But he was in a position to be perfectly misunderstood by all the various grades of his adherents in the North. In such a position as his, the true radical—not the mere conservative with a bad digestion—must feel his own way. He must constantly test out every path without losing his general direction. The people, unaccustomed to taking the long view, stick to every bypath as if it were the road to heaven. They want to think in well-rounded little categories. If through stress they are forced to adopt a new point of view—as in going from peace to war—they go body and soul, with no debatable ground, with no regard for the nice discriminations in thinking that in their total effect might some day reclaim the world. Persons accustomed to disinterested reflection may weigh matters, may be long in doubt, and finally decide that, everything considered, their country should engage in war. The unthinking politicians shake the heavens with their denunciation of the thinkers. The war comes. The politicians again shake the heavens with their denunciation of the thinkers—but this time because the thinkers dare to doubt that the enemy country cooks the grease out of its own dead soldiers to oil cannon with!

Lincoln had never hoped for the upheaval. He knew, as every thoughtful person must know, that the Civil War was one of the stupidest errors to which mankind has ever fallen a victim. But the time when it might have been avoided was long before Lincoln came to the front of the scene. By his time, there was an inevitability in events—and especially in feelings. Smaller minds jumped from one little whirlwind of an idea to another, and for the time found each one of them a complete explanation of the state of affairs. Lincoln was sensitive to the vague but unmistakable sweep of the times. Circumstances, he believed, had developed to the point where the only way out to anything better than destruction was the way of the sword. But he did not wish to use the sword so that when he had cut his way through he would find himself on the road to destruction, after all. Revolutions, he knew, had a way of departing from old lines and old laws. He must go warily on an unbroken path.

So came the holocaust of the most cruel censure a great leader has ever endured. Why not let the South go? Did he not know that a nation could not be held together by force? But if he let the South go, slavery would be more firmly established in it than ever. And the slave South, a nation in itself, would be pushed up close against the Union of the North, and would be a constant menace to free institutions. What advantage would there be in that to a man who believed slavery wrong?

But why not give the South a chance to come

back? He was ready. But he knew that the South would have to come back under the presidency of a man who stood at least for slavery's "ultimate extinction"; and he had too much of the Southerner's blood in his own veins ever to expect his contemporary slaveholders to come back peaceably on such a basis. He could with perfect candor reply to Horace Greeley: "What I do about slavery and the colored race, I do because it helps to save the Union; and what I forbear, I forbear because I do not believe it would help save the Union." For the one matter that lay behind all thought of disunion was this slave question. Had it by some sublime necromancy been settled, the Union would have been saved automatically. And the Union was now going to be saved only when his revolution against slavery became an accepted fact. Those who knew him slightly thought he was weak. But he was flexible adamant.

If he had possessed the services of one such general in 1861 as Robert E. Lee, the war might reasonably have been over within a year. The South, so hopelessly in the minority, might have been forced to accept the doctrine of "ultimate extinction"; it might have been forced to accept Lincoln's pet scheme of "compensated emancipation." In any event, he would be winning his revolution against slavery. But he had to pass through the agony of trying out generals. In the long deferred hope that he might find one who would fight, he became over-anxious and unwittingly prolonged the agony by his failure sometimes to distinguish between the function of the statesman and the function of the general.

He became the most solitary figure in the western world. Whether he looked abroad or scrutinized the landscape immediately about him, he found himself alone. In England and France men of official influence hoped the South would be victorious. It was as much, perhaps, as should have been expected of Napoleon III. He was ambitious to extend his little influence; he thought the war between the states had definitely brought to an end anything that George Washington ever did; and he could now see no good reason why France in her own interest—that is to say, in his

—should not "act accordingly," and gather up a little of the wreckage. But one might have hoped for more at the hands of an England in which Victoria and Gladstone and Lord John Russell figured so prominently—or might one? In any event, official England failed to champion Lincoln's cause. Early a few European friends like Count Agenor de Gasparin sought to enlighten England as well as France. But they were slow in producing official effect.

In his own country he was so much doubted that it is puzzling to find him able to carry on a war at all. The names he accumulated—not in the South, be it remembered, but in the North—afford a preliminary index to the esteem in which he was held. "Black Republican," "Black abolitionist," "renegade," "sectionalist," "radical," "agitator," "insurrectionist," "blatherskite," "visionary," "traitor," "revolutionist," "scoundrel," "slaughter-house Abe," "despot," "usurper," "felon," "murderer," "dirty-minded story teller," "old gorilla," "nigger-hugger," and a long list not yet considered printable in any country. His way was precarious enough, however one looked at it. In the autumn of 1862—soon after the Emancipation Proclamation was made public—an Indiana politician, writing confidentially to Senator Henry S. Lane about state and national politics, predicted that if things went on as they were going, "every state in the Union will go Democratic at the next presidential election. Mark what I say."

He could, by resorting to compulsion, command enough forces to carry on his war. But he was always surrounded by great concentric rings of skeptics. His own presidential family contained men who habitually spoke of him with contempt. The city of Washington, from members of Congress to dressmakers who made costumes for the President's wife, was an ant hill of gossip about Old Abe's predicament. One circle farther removed, the officers in the army in considerable percentage were nasty in their condemnation; and men deserted the ranks in unbelievable numbers. In the great outlying regions of the country, all sorts of men and women to whom his fight should have made appeal were either in an uproar about him or in a conspiracy against him.

Why did he not stop the insults of England and France by declaring war? Why did he not exhibit a little decision? Why did he not exhibit some of the other qualities of a leader? Even such a high-minded patriot as Charles Eliot Norton had not yet found him much of anything except woefully deficient. Norton wished Seward had been elected; he doubted whether Lincoln had a soul "open to the heats of enthusiasm for a great principle"; he saw the spectacle of "great historic deeds being accomplished, and moral principles working out their results, without one great man to do the deeds or to manifest the principle in himself." At one time he thought that unless Lincoln remade his cabinet before other military reverses came, it would be time to consider a "Committee of Safety"!

Just as many railed at him for bleeding the country to death. Why could he not be reasonable? Why did he not make peace? Had not somebody said that the South had been ready for peace all the while? Alert to every possibility to break down the North's morale, the South kept as many of these peace decoys aloft as possible. And the enemies behind the lines in the North accepted them all as very live white doves. Copperhead societies sang damnation. *The Copperhead Minstrel,* the volume of anti-Administration songs distributed throughout the country from New York City in 1863, assured Lincoln that they were coming

> *"With curses loud and deep,*
> *That will haunt you in your waking,*
> *And disturb you in your sleep."*

The entire volume was scornful enough to satisfy the most vociferous Lincoln hater of the day, and is quite incomprehensible to the Lincoln follower of the twentieth century. To the tune of "America," "patriotic families every night" were asked to sing a song beginning:

> "God save our wretched land
> From Lincoln's traitor band,
> From woe and blight."

And ending:

> "Down with the traitor band,
> The pale-faced contraband—
> White negro-knaves;
> Up with the banner bright
> Of liberty and right
> God gave to people white,
> But not to slaves."

To the tune of Lord Lovel they sang:

"Then he sent for Seward and Simon the thief,
And Welles and Bates and Blair,
To these trusty old traitors, Abe Lincoln, he said
In my new nigger kingdom you'll share—share
  —share,
In my new nigger kingdom you'll share."

And they sang every other kind of defiance and insolence:

"But crack your low jokes, Massa Lincoln,
Only white men to ruin are hurled,
So put your foot down, Massa Lincoln,
And trample them out of the world."

*"Honest Old Abe, when the war first began
Denied abolition was part of his plan;
Honest Old Abe has since made a decree
The war must go on till the slaves are all free.
As both can't be honest, will some one tell how,
If honest Abe then, he is honest Abe now?"*

From New York also emanated the publications of the *Metropolitan Record,* a press pledged to fight "fanaticism in every form." In *The Trial of Abraham Lincoln,* Lincoln was charged, in nine counts, with "treasonable intent, purposes, and designs." To the witness stand were called Washington, Jefferson, Hamilton, Jackson, Hancock, Patrick Henry, Webster, Clay, and other statesmen of the past. And they all testified against Lincoln. After the testimony, before the verdict was rendered, a great procession of the horribly disfigured, the maimed, the destitute, and the starving victims of Lincoln's "fanaticism" filed past and shrieked in agony at the defendant. Then the Spirit of the Constitution pronounced judgment, in the course of which he declared:

"You have been given the opportunity of saving a nation, but you have stabbed it to the heart. . . . To the outraged justice of your countrymen I now leave you, with the brand of *'Tyrant'* upon your brow."

The country was alive with societies—or one society under many names—designed to thwart the efforts of the President. The Knights of the Golden Circle, the Sons of Liberty, the Order of American Knights, zealously stirred up riots against the draft. They wrote letters to their neighbors in the Union army and urged them to desert— and with effect. They managed to keep in touch with Confederate authorities and receive directions from them. They helped to publish pamphlets designed to discredit everything Lincoln attempted. With more or less secrecy they carried on military drill in anticipation of "the great day"—a membership estimated at from 340,000 to 1,000,000. They nurtured a great conspiracy to free the Confederate prisoners-of-war confined in Illinois, Indiana, and Ohio. If these soldiers were unable to establish a new sister confederacy in these states, they were to return to the South and replenish the depleted armies. Confederate workers were constantly filtering down from Canada and giving encouragement to every disloyal heart.

Although Lincoln never knew on one day what friend would desert him on the next, he went his way, ever clarifying his mind in mystic communion, ever feeling ahead sensitively. They might say he had no policy if they liked; they might condemn him for having done this or not having done that; they might be tardy in inviting him to speak at Gettysburg; they might say that his manner was uncouth and his writing without style; they might—the irresponsible among them—circulate whatever lies they chose about his having been drunk on the White House lawn, having been obscene, having gone crazy. When the whole bloody business was over, there would be at least one man who would approve what he had done—the man down inside Abraham Lincoln.

In this lonely yet adequate assurance, he gave himself to the bearing of other people's burdens. He studied the cases of young boyish deserters in the army and prevented the execution of many. He heard the tearful recitals of countless widows. He heard the grievances of men wounded in battle for his ideal. He hurried back and forth between the White House and the War Department throughout the hours of every battle, and suffered with the wounded and the dying, whoever they were. "What news, my friends, what news?" he asked expectantly of the brother-in-law and sister-in-law of General Lew Wallace, as he strode into the War Department in the last hours of the battle of Shiloh. "Oh," the sister-in-law exclaimed, with a sense of relief in her voice, "we had heard that a General Wallace was among the killed, and we were afraid it was *our* Wallace. But it was not."

"Ah-h-h," he replied, looking down into her face with sad eyes; "but it was *somebody's* Wallace."

Nor was his lot much less lonely after the Union armies had begun to win. The people were tired of battles. In the early days when battles were lost everybody said, "Why doesn't Old Abe make them fight?" When he had found Grant and Sherman, everybody said, "Why doesn't Old Abe stop the awful carnage?" The people, too, were tired of hearing about negroes. What did anybody want with them now that they were free? Would Old Abe be good enough to find the answer? It was not easy. Carlyle was not only humorous but wise when he said: "The South says to the nagur, 'God bless you! and be a slave,' and the North says, 'God damn you! and be free.'"

Not even the clear assurance that Grant could not be made to run against him in 1864, not even the growing conviction that with battles won by his generals he would be reëlected, not even the good omens of every sort that daily came into view, could silence the great minority. The national convention of the opposition party was the occasion for an incidental ingathering of every kind of hater and plotter and conspirator. The free lances were out to rid the country of "tyranny." On the convention floor, if the proceedings were accurately reported, the same spirit prevailed. "They might search hell over," a delegate from Ohio declared, "and they could not find a worse President than Abraham Lincoln." Another proclaimed: "For less offenses than Mr. Lincoln has been guilty of, the English people chopped off the head of the first Charles." And still another, forerunner of the twentieth-century maker of slogans: "The people will soon rise, and if they cannot put Lincoln out of power by the ballot, they will by the bullet. (Loud cheers.)"

When the people returned him to power, he breathed an easy breath. He breathed another when he saw the end of the war only a few days ahead. Confronted with the somewhat less harrowing task of nursing a wounded nation through convalescence, he dared to hope for a little serenity. But the downward tug of his lower lip and the wistful inquiry in his gray eyes told how he would have welcomed some understanding hearts. When the news of his assassination was flashed over the country, not even the tragic manner of his going could jar the doubt—or the hatred—from the minds of tens of thousands who should have caught the spirit of his benevolent dictatorship. Senator and Mrs. Henry S. Lane, when they received the news, went down to the business section of their little Indiana town to tell as many as possible what had happened. On the way they met the pastor of the Presbyterian Church and sorrowfully broke the news to him. He was startled; but upon second thought, he believed it was providential. Lincoln had to be got out of the way so that a stronger man might grapple with the problem of reconstruction. The same morning, in an Ohio village where the same year another Republican President of the United States was born, a crowd had assembled to learn the news. When it was announced that the President had died that morning, a part of the crowd threw up their hats and shouted and went away and killed a turkey and had a celebration. "Now we'll leave the damned nigger where he belongs, and get back to the Constitution!"

The radical who had pitied the lowliest of his fellow mortals with a great love, and who early dreamed of a revolution that would set them free in an undivided American Union, had had his fling at making his contemporaries understand an ideal.

"Victory comes late."

THE END

INDEX

Académie Carmen, 76.
Academy, The, 81.
Across America and Asia, 212.
Adams, C. F., 34 *f*.
Adams, Henry, 224.
Aldrich, T. B., 256.
Alexander, J. W., 55, 57, 134.
Alexander, Mrs. J. W., 55.
"Allan Donn Puts to Sea," 138.
Alps, 92.
America, 16, 51, 54 *ff*., 58, 59, 82, 98, 103, 143, 172, 194, 238.
American Indian, 104.
American Knights, Order of, 305.
Amherst, 243, 245, 251.
Amherst College, 242.
"Amour," 138.
Anau, 219.
"Anne in White," 135.
Apaches, 204 *f*., 208, 225.
Appleton Chapel, 176 *f*.
Aral Sea, 217.
Aristophanes, 91.
Arizona, 203 *ff*.
Arnold, Matthew, 172.
Ashfield, 190.
Asia, 216 *ff*.
Atlantic Monthly, 170.
Atlantic Ocean, 52, 56, 82, 171.
"Aunt Fanny," 135, 156.

Baronet and the Butterfly, The, 53.
Bates, Edward, 291, 303.
"Battersea Bridge," 52, 64.
Battery, The, 140.
Beacon Street, 223.
Bellows, Anne, 148, 159.

Bellows, Emma (Louise Story), 148, 152, 159 *ff*.
Bellows, George, 61, 125-162.
Bellows, Jean, 148, 159.
"Benediction in Georgia," 137.
Bianchini, (   ), 104.
"Billy Sunday," 137.
Black Hawk War, 271.
Blackmore, Richard, 103.
"Blacksmith of Lyme Regis, The," 64.
Blackstone's *Commentaries*, 266.
Blair, Montgomery, 303.
Bloomington, Illinois, 280.
"Blue Snow, the Battery," 135.
Board of Overseers, Harvard, 24, 34.
Boers, 55.
Bohemia, 159.
Bonaparte, Letitia, 202.
Boston, 190, 223, 241.
Boston Common, 19.
Boston Regatta, 20.
Boston Symphony Orchestra, 99.
Bowles, Samuel, 244.
Bradstreet, Anne, 193.
Brahms, 95.
Brown, John, 169, 288 *f*.
Browning, Robert and Elizabeth Barrett, 167 *f*.
Buddha, 199.
Buffalo, 59.
Bulgaria, 45.
Bunker Hill, 235.
Burne-Jones, Edward, 52 *f*., 172.
"Business Men's Class, Y. M. C. A.," 137.

313

INDEX

Butler, N. M., 114, 116 ff.
"By the Bivouac's Fitful Flame," 156.

California, 15, 205.
Cambridge, 26, 37, 38, 168, 182, 189, 190, 196.
Cameron, Simon, 291, 303.
Carlsen, Emil, 78.
"Carlyle," 64.
Carlyle, Thomas, 91, 172, 173, 193, 308.
Carnegie Institution, 213, 219.
Carpenter, J. A., 101.
Carreño, Teresa, 99.
Cartwright, Peter, 268.
Cass, Lewis, 270.
Catholic Church, 191 f.
Catholics, 272.
Catskills, The, 145.
Celt, 103.
Cervantes, 94.
Charles I, 309.
Charleston, 169.
Chartres, Cathedral, 193.
Chase, W. M., 78.
Chelsea, 83.
Chicago, 59, 69, 100, 179.
Child, F. J., 193.
China, 31, 207, 213, 220.
Cincinnati, 288.
Circourt, Count, 167.
"City Dead House, The," 156.
Civil War, The, 183, 203, 246, 273, 294 ff.
Clay, Henry, 304.
Clemens, S. L., 94.
Cleveland, Grover, 182.
Clough, A. H., 168, 169.
Colonies, in America, 276.
Columbia University, 95, 108 ff.
Columbus, Ohio, 128, 130, 140, 157, 287.
Concord Bridge, 235.
Confederacy, The, 172.
Conrad, Joseph, 98.

Cooper Union, 289.
Copperhead Minstrel, The, 302.
Corporation, Harvard, 35.
Corsica, 199, 201 f.
Crane, Walter, 71.
Creation, 103.
"Crehaven," 135.
"Crucifixion, The," 138.
Cuba, 182.
Curtis, G. W., 172, 193.

Daggett, Mrs. Henry (George Bellows's Aunt Fanny), 148 ff.
Dakotas, The, 221.
Dallin, Cyrus, 60.
"Dance in a Mad-House," 137.
Dante, 188, 192.
Darwin, Charles, 46, 168, 172, 222.
Declaration of Independence, 282.
"Dempsey and Firpo," 137.
Dennis, John, 103.
Dickens, Charles, 172.
Dickinson, Austin, 241.
Dickinson, Edward (Father of Emily), 241 ff.
Dickinson, Emily, 233-257.
Dickinson, Emily Norcross (Mother of Emily), 241 ff.
Dickinson, Lavinia, 242, 248.
Dickinson, Susan Gilbert, 243, 244, 249.
Divina Commedia, 192.
Divinity School, Harvard, 41.
Donne, John, 193.
Don Quixote, Knight of Folly, 194.
Douglas, S. A., 261, 270, 274, 277, 279 ff.
Dred Scott decision, 273, 284.
Du Maurier, G. L. P. B., 69.
Dynamic Symmetry, 158.

East Side, The, 140.
Eden, Lady, 53.
Eden, Sir William, 53.
"Edith Cavell," 138 f.
Egypt, 167.

INDEX

"Eleanor, Jean, and Anna," 135, 148.
"Electrocution," 137.
Eliot, C. W., 13-47.
Eliot, Mrs. C. W., 25 ff., 45.
Eliot, George, 172.
Emancipation Proclamation, 300.
Emerson, R. W., 91, 193.
"Emma and Her Children," 156.
"Emma in Purple Dress," 135.
England, 51 ff., 62, 82, 83, 174, 283, 298 f., 301.
Ericsson, John, 74.
Europe, 51, 218.
Evening Post, New York, 83, 116 f.

Fabre, J. H., 253.
Faneuil Hall, 31.
Fessenden, W. P., 291.
Finck, H. T., 116.
Fireside Tales, 113.
First Parish Church, 41, 45.
Flaubert, Gustave, 98.
Florence, 167.
France, 51, 53, 56, 63, 82, 142, 298 f., 301.
Freer, C. L., 83.
Freiburg, 203.
French National Conservatory, 89.

Gaskell, Mrs. E. C., 169.
Gasparin, Count Agenor de, 299.
Gentle Art of Making Enemies, The, 63.
Georgia, 189.
Germany, 89, 99.
Gettysburg, 306.
Glackens, W. J., 144.
Gladstone, W. E., 299.
Gobi Desert, 208.
Godkin, E. L., 182.
Goethe, 193.
Gogebic iron region, 214.
Grant, U. S., 308.
Greece, 187.
Greeley, Horace, 279, 297.

Green Mountains, 231.
Grieg, Edvard, 105.
Grosvenor, H. C., 204.

Hague, J. D., 224.
Hakodate, 206.
Hals, Frans, 160.
Hambidge, Jay, 158.
Hamerton, Philip, 70.
Hamilton, Alexander, 304.
Hancock, John, 304.
Harper's Magazine, 69, 287.
Harrison, Frederic, 172.
Harvard Law School, 35.
Harvard Medical School, 21, 34 f.
Harvard Memories, 34 f.
Harvard Square, 38.
Harvard Union, 178.
Harvard University, 20, 109, 175 ff., 178, 179, 183, 213.
Hawthorne, C. W., 60.
Heart of Oak Books, 193.
Henri, Robert, 60, 131, 159, 161.
Henry, Patrick, 304.
Herndon, W. H., 278.
Herodotus, 91.
Higginson, T. W., 244, 245, 254.
Hillcrest, 94.
Hoar, G. F., 184.
Holland, Mr. and Mrs. J. G., 244.
Holmes, O. W., 47.
Holt, Henry, 224.
Holy Ghost Hospital, 191 f., 196.
Hospital Aid Society, 192.
Hound of Heaven, 255.
Huddleston, Baron, 52.
Hudson River, 140.
Huneker, James, 113.
Hunt, Helen, 244.
Huxley, T. H., 222.
Hylan, J. F., 144.

Illinois, 168, 169, 265, 268, 276, 277, 279 ff., 286, 292.
India, 166.
Indian, American, 199.
Indian Suite, 113.

INDEX

Indiana, 264, 291.
Indianapolis, 59.
"Initiation in the Frat," 137.
Iowa, 221.

Jackson, Andrew, 304.
James, Henry, 51.
James, William, 184 *f*.
Japan, 206.
Jefferies, Richard, 91.
Jefferson, Thomas, 269, 304.
Jehovah, 199.
Jenny Lind, 246.
Jesus of Nazareth, 267.
Jesus, Gospel Story of birth of, 27, 188.
Johnson, Samuel, 103.
Joullin, Amédée, 78.

Kansas, 189.
Karakul, Lake, 231.
Keltic Sonata, 105, 113.
Kentucky, 280 *f*.
King, Clarence, 224.
Kipling, Rudyard, 155, 193.
Knights of the Golden Circle, The, 305.
Know-Nothings, 272.

La Farge, John, 60.
"La Mère Gérard," 65.
"La Princesse du Pays de la Porcelaine," 64.
"Lady Jean," 135, 156.
Lake Superior, 228.
Lamartine, Alphonse de, 167.
Lane, H. S., 290 *ff*., 300, 309 *f*.
Lane, Mrs. H. S., 309.
"Law is Too Slow, The," 137.
Leavenworth, Kansas, 288.
Leaves of Grass, 266.
Lee, R. E., 297.
Leighton, Lord, 82.
Leonardo da Vinci, 139.
Lewes, G. H., 172, 173.
Leyland, F. R., 53.

Library of Congress, 84.
"Lillie in Our Alley," 64.
Lincoln, Abraham, 154, 168, 169 *f*., 259-311.
"Little Blue Bonnet, The," 65.
Liverpool, 57.
Livy, 91.
Log Cabin, MacDowell's, 111.
London, 51, 55, 57, 58, 62, 63, 64, 241.
London, Jack, 155.
Longfellow, H. W., 166, 168.
Lord, O. P., 244.
Low, Seth, 113, 121.
Lowell, J. R., 166, 168, 170, 193.
Lowell, Massachusetts, 54, 85.
Loyal Publication Society, 170.
Lucretius, 103.
Luxembourg Garden, 57.
Luxembourg Museum, 64, 150.
Lyon, Mary, 235.

MacDowell, Edward, 87-123, 145.
Macleod, Fiona, 91, 105.
Maha Rajah Apurva Krishna Bahadoor, 166.
Malory, Thomas, 91.
Mark Twain, 93.
Massachusetts Historical Society, 22.
Massachusetts Institute of Technology, 20.
Masses, The, 141.
Mateo Falcone, 201.
Mauclair, Camille, 75.
Maupassant, Guy de, 108.
McClure's Magazine, 66.
Mediterranean Sea, 201.
Memorial Hall, 42, 178.
Menominee iron region, 214.
Mephistopheles, 62.
Mérimée, Prosper, 201.
Methodists, 153.
Metropolitan Record, 304.
Mexicans, 204.
Mexico, 183, 272 *f*., 277.

INDEX

Michael Angelo, 146, 160.
Michigan, 214.
Mill, J. S., 172.
Minnesota, 132.
Mississippi River, 230.
Mississippi Valley, 94, 248.
Missouri, 214, 221.
Missouri Compromise, 284.
Monadnock, Mount, 231.
Mongolia, 213, 220.
Montclair, 62.
Morley, John, 172.
Morning Advertiser, 81.
Morris, William, 172.
Moscow, 209.
Moses, 146, 199.
"Mother," 64, 82, 85.
Mount Holyoke Female Seminary, 235.
Mozart, 108.
Museum of Comparative Zoölogy, 178.

Napoleon I, 202.
Napoleon III, 298.
Nation, The, 171, 181, 182.
National Academy of Design, 134, 142.
National Arts Club, 138.
National Board of Health, 214.
New England, 92.
New England Idyls, 113.
New Hampshire, 90.
New York, 56, 58, 66, 83, 90, 130, 140, 145, 157, 179, 241, 261, 279, 302.
New York School of Art, 131.
Niagara Falls, 180.
"Nocturne in Black and Gold," 52.
Noeggerath, J. J., 202 *f.*
Norcross, Fannie, 244.
Norcross, Louisa, 244.
Norse Sonata, 113.
North American Review, 170 *f.,* 181.
North Pole, 16.

Northampton, 246.
Northern Transcontinental Survey, 215.
Northwest Territory, 284.
Norton, Charles Eliot, 27, 163-196, 301.
Norton's Pride, 177.

"O Captain, My Captain," 156.
Ohio, 291, 309, 310.
Ohio State University, 128 *ff.*
"Old Billiard Player," 137.
Orient, 224 *f.*

Pacific Ocean, 224.
Paderewski, Ignace, 94, 101.
Pamir, 231.
Paris, 63, 75, 78, 89, 167, 241.
Parkman, Francis, 109.
Peabody, F. G., 27.
Peacock Room, 53, 85.
Pennell, Joseph, 138, 145.
Pennell, Joseph and Elizabeth Robins, 82, 84.
Pennington, William, 291.
Peterboro, 96, 111.
Petrograd, 210.
Philadelphia, 250.
Pinochle Palace, 66.
Pittsburgh, 59.
Poet Gray as a Naturalist, The, 193.
Polk, J. K., 272 *ff.*
Pond, J. B., 57.
Pope, The, 39.
"Portrait of F. R. Leyland," 65.
"Portrait of Katherine Rosen," 135.
"Portrait of M. Théodore Duret," 65.
"Portrait of My Mother," 135.
"Portrait of Walter Hampden," 144.
Poston, C. D., 205.
Pozzo di Borgo family, 201 *f.*
"President Grant" architecture, 165.

INDEX

Princeton, 178.
Pumpelly, Raphael, 197-231.
"Punchinello in the House of Death," 138.
Puritans, 103, 237 ff., 249 ff.

Queen Victoria, 15, 161, 299.
Quincy, 34 f.
Quincy Street, 37 f.

Rachel, Mlle., 167 f.
Raff, J. J., 89, 121.
"Reducing," 137.
Reminiscences, of Raphael Pumpelly, 201, 212.
Republican, Springfield, 247.
"Return to Life, The," 138.
Richthofen, Ferdinand von, 220.
Rocky Mountains, 215.
Rome, 169.
Roof of the World, 231.
Roosevelt, Theodore, 32.
Royal Mining Academy, 203.
Royal Poet of Delhi, 166, 168.
Royal Society of British Artists, 53.
Ruskin, John, 52 ff., 62, 64, 72, 169, 171 ff.
Russell, Lord John, 299.
Russia, 85, 220, 272.

Sahara Desert, 203.
Samoan Islands, 108.
San Francisco, 206.
Schiller, 91.
Schopenhauer, 253.
Sea Pieces, 113.
Seward, W. H., 170, 291 f., 301, 303.
Shady Hill, 168, 188, 191, 196.
Shanghai, 207.
"Sharkey's," 135.
Sherman, W. T., 308.
"Shower-Bath, The," 137.
Siberia, 208 ff.
Sibley, Joe, 69.

"Sixteen East Gay Street," 137.
Skyscrapers, 101.
Smithsonian Institution, 213.
Society of Perfect Wives and Husbands, 161.
"Song of the Graduates," 55.
Sons of Liberty, The, 305.
Sophocles, 91.
Spain, 182.
Speed, J. F., 271.
Speed, John, 290.
Spot Resolutions, 272.
"Spring, Gramercy Park," 135.
St. James, Court of, 46.
St. Paul, Minnesota, 70.
St. Peter, 176.
Stephen, Leslie, 172.
Story, Emma Louise, 133.
Strong, Mrs. Annie P., 245.
Sun, New York, 68.
Sunday, Billy, 135.
Supreme Court, 273 ff., 287.
Symphony, Boston, 39.

Taylor, J. R., 130.
Taylor, Tom, 53.
"Ten O'Clock," 57 f., 62, 70, 85.
Thames, 57, 68, 74.
Tharaud, Jean, 56.
Thomas, Theodore, 109, 114.
Times, New York, 101.
Tinlot, Hon. Dicky Peachblow, 66.
Tolstoy, 91.
Tories, 276.
Trial of Abraham Lincoln, The, 304.
Tribune, New York, 64.
Trilby, 69, 77.
Turkestan, 218 ff., 228.

United States, 15, 52, 60, 89, 189, 221.
United States Embassy, 84.
University Hall, 28, 37.
Upper Montclair, 133.

INDEX

Vasari's *Lives of the Painters*, 91.
Velasquez, 67, 74.
Venezuela, 182.
Venice, 66, 74, 167.
Victorian Era, 16.
Vienna, 202.
"Village Prayer Meeting," 137.
Villard, Henry, 215 *f*.
Villari's *Life and Times of Machiavelli*, 91.
Virginia, 280.
Virginie, 167.
Vita Nuova, 193.

Wagner, Richard, 95, 115.
Wallace, Lew, 307.
Washington, D. C., 60, 85, 294, 300.
Washington, George, 298, 304.
Washington's Birthday, 1842, 265.
Webster, Daniel, 304.

Weismann, August, 108.
West Point, 54 *f*.
Whistler, J. M., 49-85, 145.
"White Girl," 54, 64.
Whitman, Walt, 89, 155 *f*., 168, 266.
Whitney, Maria, 244.
Whittier, J. G., 46 *f*.
Wilde, Oscar, 54, 62, 68.
Wilson, Woodrow, 91.
"With Husky Haughty Lips, O Sea," 156.
Woodberry, G. E., 116.
Woodbury, C. H., 60.
World Court, 17.
World War, 142.

Yale University, 23, 178.
Yangtze-Kiang, 207.
Yard, Harvard, 39, 44.
"Yellow Buskin, The," 65.
Yellow Sea, 207.